WHAT ABOUT FACE?
How I Gave Up My Broken Dreams

Jad and Rachelle Terrebonne
with Amy Terrebonne Luarca

It's about the
Journey

DEDICATION

This book is dedicated to my dad who is now in Heaven and to my son Paul.

To Dad, thank you for all of the fishing and hunting trips we took together. You did not realize that all the times we had together in the great outdoors taught me how big God is. You are my all-time hero. I love you.

To Paul, my beloved son, thank you for being the best Bible teacher I have ever had. Truly God has manifested His works in your life. Although we have not enjoyed all of the things that most fathers and sons do together, I love you just the way you are.

– Jad Terrebonne

Copyright © 2010

For Additional Copies, Please Contact:

JAD AND RACHELLE TERREBONNE
whataboutpaul@yahoo.com
Web Site: Available on
Amazon.com
ISBN: 978-0-615-35217-6

Cover Credits:
Photo Cover: Courtesy of Larry Titak Photography
Family Picture: Picture People
Cover Design: Jad Terrebonne

All Scriptures are from the King James Bible.

Printed and Bound in the United States

ACKNOWLEDGMENTS

I WANT TO THANK some very special people.

Rick Bartley, thank you for not being ashamed of reading your Bible in front of everyone at the Navy dispensary. I am on my way to Heaven because of you.

Brother Wesly Millard, my former pastor, thank you for all of your encouragement, wisdom, and warmhearted preaching. You were a very special mentor. You and your wife are two of the most beautiful people in the world.

Tom Atchison, thank you for all of your knowledge and wisdom in guiding us through the maze of rules and regulations with which we had to deal regarding Paul.

John and Diane Wilson, thank you for your dedication to helping Paul and the other Pathfinders (educably slow adults) of First Baptist Church of Hammond. You are gifts from God.

Dr. Jack Hyles and Dr. Jack Schaap, thank you for your love for the Pathfinders. Because of you, they have a church they can call home.

Ben Walkup, thank you for being Paul's Sunday school teacher all these years.

Linda Stubblefield and Rena Fish, thank you for helping to make this book a reality.

Mom, you're wonderful. Thank you for being such a great cook. I love you dearly.

Amy and Daniel, thank you for being a wonderful daughter and son-in-law. May you always do God's will for your life.

Rachelle, my wife, thank you for your faithfulness all these years. All of the trials and heartaches you faced have not diminished the beauty of your smile. Thank you for your never-ending encouragement to me. I love you dearly.

– Jad Terrebonne

CONTENTS

INTRODUCTION

JAD AND RACHELLE Terrebonne are two of the finest Christians I pastor in a church full of truly great Christians. They have two beautiful adult children, a lovely daughter Amy and a precious son Paul. This book is about Paul, a mentally handicapped young man of 27 years. This book is an insider's look at a couple and a family as they wrestled with the many realities facing similar families.

Their dreams, disappointments, frustrations, and victories are chronicled in this book and will challenge your spirit, humble your pride, and bring you into a greater understanding of families that must live daily with tough choices. With special chapters by the father, mother, and sister, we the readers gain a keen insight and a valuable perspective.

I love this family with all my heart. Through heartaches, disappointed dreams, brain surgery for Rachelle, and countless agonizing moments with Paul, the Terrebonnes are a family whose tenacity and devotion I have grown to respect.

– Pastor Jack Schaap
First Baptist Church
Hammond, Indiana

FOREWORD

IT IS WONDERFUL to see how God has been and is now using Paul Terrebonne's life to bring glory to Himself through this captivating book of Paul's life. The heartaches, the struggles, the uncertainties, as well as the victories and God's grace written down in this book are a testimony of the strength of faith the Terrebonne family has and is exhibiting in God Almighty.

It has been an honor for me to review this book and once again see how our Heavenly Father molds our lives through the valleys and the trials that we might come forth as gold. As I read this book, it was a heartwarming reminder that God delights in using what the world calls "unlovely."

As you read this book, there will be a twofold effect; it will tug at your heart and bless your soul.

– Dr. Tom Williams, President
Tom Williams Evangelistic Ministries
Belt, Montana

1

BORN ON THE BAYOU

W E SIPPED HOT coffee as we sat together in our duck blind. The decoys floated in the pond filled with the reflections of the moon and stars. Soon the sun would rise over this majestic Louisiana swamp.

With my new Winchester 20-gauge shotgun, I entered into another part of Dad's world. This world was not only a world of duck hunting and fishing; this was a world built on love, trust, and admiration for a man who was bigger than life to a young boy. Yes, I was thrilled to own my new gun. But the day he handed it to me one December night, Dad handed me his trust. With that trust, he allowed me to take one more step to manhood.

I was born on the bayou in Houma, Louisiana. Terrebonne Parish General Hospital opened its doors on July 13, 1954, as a 65-bed hospital, and on August 26, 1954, I was born into the family of Jack and Juanita Terrebonne. Across the street from the hospital where I was born is Bayou Terrebonne. Over the course of

Jack & Juanita Terrebonne

Above: The hospital where my sisters and I were born
Below (left to right): Jad, Jacqueline (in walker), Glynis,
and Robin (standing behind Jacqueline)

several years, my three sisters, Glynis, Robin, and Jacqueline were all born at the same hospital. After a few days, I was taken home to the small fishing community of Cypremort Point, Louisiana. There, Dad and my grandfather ran a seafood business. They owned two shrimp boats, the *Wilma* and a white schooner named the *Jerry and Ray.*

The blessing of the fleet marked the beginning of shrimp season. Each year the fishermen decorated their boats with flags and streamers and then proceeded down the bayou for the blessings of the local Catholic priest. It was an event celebrated with lots of music and hearty Cajun cooking.

The shrimp season was filled with long hours trawling the waters of Vermillion Bay and finished with more long hours of the fishermen's unloading their catch at the docks of my family's business. I still remember Mom's cooking dinner and serving the workers on the back porch of our house. Dinner was usually a big pot of white beans and rice with fried shrimp followed by a large glass of sweet tea.

Six-year-old Jad

Life for us was simple and rugged, and we enjoyed the bounty of the land on which we lived. We had a garden for fresh vegetables and a hen house for eggs. The chicken for dinner was the one that didn't get away. Every fall we butchered a hog and made delicious boudin, smoked sausage, hog head cheese, and pork roasts. The month of October signaled the begin-

A shrimp boat on the bayou

ning of the oyster harvest. Raw oysters are still one of my favorite foods.

Just as the shrimp season was coming to a close, it was time to go hunting. Dad always brought home a variety of game including ducks, coots, rabbits, and deer. Sometimes he took me for a drive on the highway to shoot rabbits off the side of the road. The words "game warden" were spoken in hushed tones because no one bothered to obtain a hunting license and your limit was filled when you ran out of shotgun shells. The season ended when everyone got tired of hunting.

This simple life taught me to enjoy the great outdoors. I always looked forward to Dad's taking me fishing out in the bay. I learned how to catch speckled trout before I learned how to read.

Whenever I wasn't fishing with Dad, I was playing with my toy pirogue and our dog Zoro in the ditch next to our house. We also played inside of a small log cabin that Dad and my grandfather built for us.

The pirogue Dad built for me

We enjoyed picking blackberries that grew abundantly during the summer. Glynis and I would mash a bowl full of them with sugar and eat them. After we finished eating the blackberries, we would drink from the bottom of the bowl the remaining juice that left us with purple mustaches on our top lips. Mom made preserves and dumplings with the blackberries.

The men took the rest of the berries to make homemade blackberry wine. During the winter, Mom gave us a small glass of this wine whenever my sister and I caught a bad cold. She then rubbed our chests with Vicks VapoRub. The wine might not have cured our colds, but we enjoyed a good night's sleep. You might say that it was good old-fashioned "Cajun Nyquil."

Down the road from our business was the Blue Moon Restaurant. The building had a tin roof and large screened windows with ceiling fans. The inside of the restaurant was filled with picnic tables. People from out of town went there to eat boiled crabs and shrimp. And for a nickel in the jukebox, the patrons listened to the popular two-step Cajun music.

Our music was a big part of our culture. Just imagine eating a boiled crab as you listened to PeeWee Broussard sing the "New Iberia Stomp." And as you bit into a boiled potato, the air was filled with the music of great recording artists like Rufus Thibodeaux singing "Mean Old Audrey," Blackie Fruge and the Moonlight Serenaders with their hit song "La Robe Barre," Jake and Charlie Broussard and the Midnight Ramblers crooning their title song "Two Step de Grand Lac," along with the ever popular Balfa Brothers playing "Petite Galop pour Mamou."

I have fond memories of going to my grandfather's house on a Saturday afternoon and watching many of these singers on KLFY-TV out of Lafayette, Louisiana. I never understood

My family (left to right): Glynis, Juanita Terrebonne, Jacqueline, Robin, and I am standing.

the French words that they sang, but their music knitted my heart to our Cajun way of life.

HURRICANE AUDREY

On June 25, 1957, during another busy shrimp season, a small tropical storm entered the Gulf of Mexico from the Atlantic Ocean. On June 26, Hurricane Audrey was the first category 2 storm of the Atlantic hurricane season. By the next day, it was already classed as a category 4 hurricane with peak winds of 145 miles per hour. Waves 20 feet high were reported in the Gulf of Mexico.

With Audrey's bearing down on Cypremort Point, we quickly packed our belongings and evacuated the area. Within a few hours, my family faced an uncertain future.

In Cameron, Louisiana, waves as high as ten feet were reported. In Lake Charles a storm tide of seven feet was recorded while surges up to twelve feet were reported in other locations. My grandfather's house, which was sitting on four-foot concrete pillars, was filled with almost six feet of water. My parents' house next door fared even worse and was nearly covered with water. The storm was so powerful that it pushed the tidal surge twenty-five miles inland. Miraculously both houses were still standing after the hurricane.

The damage in Louisiana was so devastating that it left between 60 to 80 percent of all businesses and homes from Cameron to Grand Chenier either destroyed or damaged. At least 600 people were killed in Texas and Louisiana with over 40,000 people left homeless. Hurricane Audrey left the equivalent of over one billion dollars in today's economy ($147 million 1957 USD) in damage.

While moving inland, Audrey spawned 23 tornadoes, which killed two people and injured fourteen in Mississippi and Alabama while causing $600,000 (1957 USD) in damage. When the storm entered the Ohio valley, it merged with another storm causing severe rain and flooding, killing ten people. In Pennsylvania the storm generated winds up to 65 mph. New York reported winds from between 95 to 100 hundred miles per hour. When the storm finally dissipated over Canada, it had sustained winds up to 80 miles per hour.

The name Audrey was retired and never again used to name a hurricane. With over 600 people killed, Audrey is ranked as the sixth deadliest hurricane to strike the United States mainland since accurate storm recording started in 1900. No future hurricane caused as many deaths in the United States until Katrina in 2005.

When it was all over, Audrey destroyed our family's seafood business. For three years Dad and my grandfather worked hard to rebuild the business. Many of the fishermen who lost their boats and houses relocated elsewhere. Our family was never able to fully recover from the devastation, and the bills began to pile up. Within three years after Audrey, the "Jack Terrebonne Seafood" business ended in bankruptcy. A year later my grandfather died of a heart attack.

Out of this tragedy, Dad converted his white schooner, the *Jerry and Ray* into a tugboat. After several months of study, he passed the Coast Guard exams and became a licensed tugboat captain. Our lives, it seemed, would be always tied to the delta waters of Louisiana.

Post-Audrey Cypremort Point gradually changed from a hub for the seafood business to a place of tourism and sport fishing. With this change, Mom decided it was time to move. One day when Dad was out on his tugboat, Mom hired a few men to help us move to another town. Dad returned home that day to an empty house and learned that we had moved to the town of Jeanerette. We lived there for a year and then moved to the town of Franklin.

Dad used his tugboat to push barges up and down the Mississippi River and through the Intracostal Canal. The *Jerry and Ray* was a sturdy tugboat, but it did not have the capacity to compete with the larger riverboats on the Mississippi River. Dad was unable to keep the business profitable and maintain the constant repairs the boat needed. He sold the boat and used the money to buy a new house in Houma, Louisiana.

Soon after we moved back to my hometown, Dad landed a job working for the U.S. Corps of Engineers as a boat operator. He was assigned to a crew that was responsible for spraying the water lilies that clogged the bayous and canals of the region. He left for work on Monday morning and did not return home until Friday afternoon.

Seven years after Audrey, we went from being "out-in-the-sticks" Cajuns to small-town suburbanites. My sisters and I learned an all new way of life. Bye-bye chickens running around the yard; we had to buy them without feathers at the store. The hen house for eggs was now next to the milk at the supermarket. Pork chops no longer had four legs; they were neatly wrapped in the meat department. For the first time ever, Mom brought home frozen pizza for supper. And when we caught a cold, we bought our medicine at the drugstore. Our Cajun Nyquil was a "medicine" of the past.

Life in our neighborhood remained simple. The vacant lot

in front of the subdivision was our favorite place to play baseball and fly kites and model airplanes. My sisters soon made new friends at school as well as around the neighborhood.

What did not change was our love for fishing and trawling for shrimp. It wasn't long after we moved into our new house before Dad bought a small aluminum boat. I was a bayou boy once again as Dad and I enjoyed many years of fishing together.

One day one of the local doctors asked Dad to spray the lilies that were growing in some of the swampland that he leased for duck hunting. In exchange for this favor, he allowed us to hunt on his property. This was the beginning of another facet of our relationship together.

As a young boy, I had longed for the day when I was able to go hunting with Dad. One of my uncles loaned us a single barrel .410 gauge shotgun. I read books from the library about gun safety. In the fall, we took the gun with us on fishing trips. There he taught me how to shoot marsh hens as they walked along the side of the bayou.

On the night of December 8, 1967, Dad walked into the kitchen of our house and handed me a brand new Winchester Model 1400 automatic 20-gauge shotgun. While admiring my new shotgun, I joined yet another part of my father's world.

The sun was now rising as we finished our coffee and waited for our first hunt together to begin. It wasn't long after Dad started calling them in that the ducks started flying into our decoys. My first shots with my new gun missed their mark. But looking back, it didn't matter because I was with Dad. It took several hunts with him to get used to my new gun. With practice I became a good shot and enjoyed the companionship of my father on our many duck hunts together.

After a few years, Dad went to Davidson's Hardware store and bought a new Browning Belgian-made A-5 20-gauge shotgun. While we drove home that day, he said, "I am going to give this gun to my first grandson." From that moment on, I dreamed of the day when I would hand that gun to my own son. He paid $235.50 for it, and today it is worth over $1,100. I also have the original box and owner's manual that came with the gun.

The hardware store where Dad bought the Browning

We were finishing an afternoon duck hunt together as the sun began to set. Storm clouds were gathering quickly, and the sound of thunder roared as the sky flashed with lightning. The rain and cloud cover reduced our ability to see. I knew this trip home would be dangerous.

As we entered the Intracoastal Canal, I saw the running lights of the passing tugboats. Dad turned on our spotlight to let them know of our presence. This very active and hazardous canal supports a large part of the maritime industry of Louisiana, Texas, and Florida. I knew that any navigational error on Dad's part would cause a deadly collision with the titans of this commercial waterway. Our little boat bounced hard against the wake created by these giant boats.

Within a few minutes after the rain started, we were soaking wet in spite of the rain gear we were wearing. Because of the cold, I turned my back to the wind and rain. When I looked up, I barely saw the shadow of my father against the night sky. Dad's experience as a tugboat captain helped guide us safely through this stormy night.

When we finally arrived home, Mom had supper waiting for us. After we changed into some dry clothes, we sat down to eat at the kitchen table. When I looked across the table, I no longer saw only the shadow of my father; I saw him face to face. I did not realize that night that one day I was going to need a Heavenly Father to guide me through an even darker night.

A World War II ship with the name Terrebonne.

2

COLLEGE AND THE NAVY

A FTER I GRADUATED from high school, I attended Nicholls State University and majored in Marine Biology and Art. While attending classes, I met a fellow student from my high school days named Randy. As we talked, I noticed a small building named "Baptist Student Union." He told me he was a member and invited me in. We chatted for a few minutes before I left for another class. But for some reason the words "Baptist Student Union" kept attracting my attention.

Terrebonne High School, the high school I attended

When I first met Randy in high school, I knew that something was different about him. For one thing, he always had a short haircut and wore long-sleeved shirts. I thought that something about his religion kept him from wearing short-sleeved shirts. He had a quiet personality and stayed to himself. I did not realize then that he belonged to a Baptist church. The fact that he was a Christian captured my attention.

In 1974 I decided to join the Navy after visiting the recruiting office in town. As I looked through the Navy career

Above: The Baptist Student Union today
Below: Nicholls State University campus

catalog, I decided to become a hospital corpsman. Although my dad was not happy about my joining the Navy, he seemed content about the idea of my becoming a hospital corpsman.

The recruiter gave me a bus ticket to New Orleans for my physical exam. I failed my first physical because of a perforated eardrum. Two surgeries later, I was able to pass the physical exam and enlisted in the Navy.

While I was waiting for my final physical exam, a man with the Gideons International organization was handing out New Testaments. He gave a short message and asked if anyone wanted a New Testament. Something compelled me to take one. It was the first time I had ever owned a copy of the King James Bible. On the bus ride home, I opened the Testament and read from Revelation 10:8-10, *"And the voice I heard from heaven spake unto me again, and said, Go and take the little book which is open in the hand of the angel which standeth upon the sea and upon the earth. And I went unto the angel, and said unto him, Give me the little book. And he said unto me, Take it, and eat it up; and it shall make thy belly bitter, but it shall be in thy mouth sweet as honey. And I took the little book out of the angel's hand, and ate it up; and it was in my mouth sweet as honey: and as soon as I had eaten it, my belly was bitter."*

At the time I did not understand the meaning of those verses, but I know the Gideons representative who gave me the New Testament was sent from God. I was now on a journey that was going to lead me to understand the meaning of those verses.

After I enlisted, I was sent to Orlando, Florida, for boot camp. It was August, and the humidity was at its worst.

Although it was tough, boot camp gave me a lot of self-confidence and taught me the importance of teamwork.

Upon graduating from boot camp, I was transferred to the Naval School of Health Sciences in San Diego, California. I enjoyed the classes and did well enough to be promoted to Third Class Petty Officer.

After graduation I was given orders to report to the U.S. Naval Hospital in Beaufort, South Carolina. I was allowed to take two weeks of leave, so I flew home to Louisiana.

After my leave was over, I boarded a plane in New Orleans and flew to the Atlanta International Airport. I switched planes in Atlanta and flew to Savannah, Georgia. It was late in the evening when I arrived, and I checked into a motel for the night. The next morning I called a cab to take me to the bus station.

When the cab driver arrived, he offered to take me to Beaufort for $20. I tossed my sea bag into the back seat of the taxi, and we were off to Beaufort. The scenery was beautiful. Oak trees with moss hanging from the branches lined the highway.

We finally arrived at the hospital; I checked in with the chief of the day. Once I was checked in, I was assigned a room in the barracks.

The next day I joined several other new hospital corpsmen for orientation to the hospital. I was then assigned to work on the inpatient surgical unit, B-3. I worked on this unit for nine months and acquired many new skills in patient care. It was my first experience in dealing with Marine Corps recruits.

The Naval hospital where I was stationed was commissioned on May 1, 1949, on 127 acres of land, and the first patient was admitted on May 5, 1949. The site, which was once the John Joiner Smith Plantation, included Camp Saxton, a Civil War garrison, and Fort Frederick. The English built Fort Beaufort in 1735 to protect the city of Beaufort from the Native Americans in the area as well as from the Spaniards to the south. The remains of its walls stand within the Naval hospital compound as a duly designated historical monument.

Nine months after I arrived at the hospital, I was transferred to Parris Island, the famous recruit training center for the Marine Corps. I was cross-trained in most of the departments and assigned to be the assistant petty officer in charge of sick call.

I enjoyed the opportunity to work with the doctors, and I learned how to obtain the medical history of the young Marine Corps recruits we examined every day.

My chief petty officer was a real motivator and mentor. After several months he let me run the clinic while he sat at the front desk. From time to time he checked on me but had confidence in me to oversee the rest of the corpsmen assigned to our department.

Although I was stationed on Parris Island, I still lived in the barracks at the main hospital and ate my meals at the hospital chow hall. During one evening chow, I happened to meet Chaplain Dennis. I was already impressed with his kindness to the Marine recruits while I was working on the surgical unit at the hospital. As we talked, he invited me to Sunday morning chapel services. For some reason, I decided to accept his invitation.

On Sunday morning at least a dozen people were in attendance. This was the first non-Catholic church service I had attended. Chaplain Dennis had everyone open a hymn book and sing several songs before he delivered his morning sermon. After everyone finished singing, he opened his Bible and read from John 8:32, *"And ye shall know the truth, and the truth shall make you free."* Several of the statements he made during his message caught my attention. He stated that the truth will not always make life easy for you, but it will always make you free. He also explained that living the truth will not make you popular or win new friends, but it will always make you free. At the end of the service, I stood up and said to myself, "Whatever the truth is that he is talking about, I am going to find it." I was getting closer to the answers of the "little book" in the book of Revelation.

It was near the end of a typical day in the dispensary. Most of the recruits who needed medical attention returned to their platoons. One or two of them were left standing outside the doctor's office waiting to be seen. I was busy with my men, cleaning the examining rooms and waiting for the watch to be set.

Just before the watch was set, Rick Bartley came walking down the hall carrying his big black Bible. Several of the other corpsmen started snickering quietly to themselves. "There goes Mr. Bible." He was tall, and his dark beard and hair seemingly made his ears stick out, but what grabbed my attention was his big black Bible. He seemed to carry it with him all of the time. On top of that, he did not seem bothered by the other men who were making fun of him. I was also impressed whenever I saw him reading from the Bible during the evenings we were on duty together. During chow one evening when several of the men were making fun of Rick and his Bible-thumping ways, I spoke up and said, "You can say whatever you want to say about him, but at least the man is sincere."

After chow was over, I walked over to sick call and opened a filing cabinet and found a black Gideon Bible. It was my turn for the pharmacy watch that night. I picked up the Bible and went back to the pharmacy. While I sat at the desk, I began turning through its pages and found Deuteronomy 4:29, *"But if from thence thou shalt seek the LORD thy God, thou shalt find him, if thou seek him with all thy heart and with all thy soul."* This verse grabbed my attention, and I prayed, "Dear God, show me the meaning of this verse."

I stood up from the desk, leaned my head against the wall, and prayed again. "Dear God, I do believe in You."

Another week or two went by when I was working in medical records. Sometime during the day, I heard the mention of Hal Lindsay's book, *The Late Great Planet Earth.* I scribbled the name of it on a piece of paper and went to the local library the following Saturday to check it out.

I could not put his book down. I was amazed at his Biblical explanations about the present and future events in the world. Lindsay wrote about the rise of Russia and her alliance with the Arab world. In chapter three, he addressed the fulfillment of the prophecies of Jesus Christ; His virgin birth; His death, burial, and resurrection; along with the future of Israel as a nation. Throughout the book, Lindsay spoke of the end times and the second coming of Jesus Christ at the Rapture.

Finally in the last chapter, he spelled out the plan of salvation and addressed the message of Revelations 3:20, *"Behold, I stand at the door, and knock: if any man hear my voice, and open the door, I will come in to him, and will sup with him, and he with me.*" At that point, God opened my eyes to the Gospel of Jesus Christ. Suddenly, everything all made sense. I realized getting to Heaven was as easy as trusting Christ in your heart as the only way to get to Heaven. The "little book" about which I had read in Revelation chapter ten was the Word of God. I do not remember the exact prayer I prayed. All I remember is bowing my head that day and believing that Jesus Christ is indeed the Son of God.

On the following Sunday, I was invited to attend the Port Royal Baptist Church outside the gate of the hospital by a lady stationed at our hospital. Rick Bartley invited me to attend his church, but the idea of having a date and attending church at the same time seemed more appealing. After the pastor delivered his sermon, I felt compelled to go forward during the invitation. When I reached the front of the auditorium, the pastor shook my hand and asked me why I was coming forward. All I could say was, "Sir, I am saved."

He asked me two more questions: "Do you believe in Calvary?" and "Do you believe that Jesus rose from the dead?"

I answered, "Sir, with all my heart and all my soul, I believe in Jesus Christ."

On Monday I couldn't wait to tell Rick what had happened to me on Sunday. We both rejoiced together and became good friends. Now two of us at the dispensary carried our Bibles to work.

During this time, I received orders to attend laboratory assistant school in Portsmouth, Virginia. I flew home for two weeks of leave, then returned to Beaufort to get my car and drive to Virginia. Rick was kind enough to help me find a good church to attend while I was in lab school.

For the few months I was in Portsmouth, I attended Temple Baptist Church in Chesapeake, Virginia. During a missions conference, the main speaker preached from the text in Isaiah 6:8, *"Also I heard the voice of the Lord, saying, Whom shall I send, and who will go for us? Then said I, Here am I; send me."* During the invitation, I went forward to surrender my life to serve God.

When I graduated from lab school, I was transferred to Jacksonville, North Carolina, for field medical technician school. There I learned how to treat casualties during combat situations. Upon completion of school, I returned to Beaufort, South Carolina. After I arrived in Beaufort, I joined the Victory Baptist Church, and life for me began to change.

Before I left for Virginia, Rick gave me a cassette tape with two sermons by Dr. Jack Hyles, the pastor of First Baptist Church of Hammond, Indiana. One sermon was entitled, "I Will Not Leave You As Orphans," and the other sermon was "Seven Steps to Success." I played these two sermons until the tape was literally worn out. Pastor Jack Hyles soon became one of my favorite preachers.

Our church was still meeting at the Shell Point Elementary School while we were in a building program. It wasn't long after I joined the church that I became involved with the bus routes and Sunday school programs. Working in these avenues taught me how to go soul winning. Pastor Millard was a warmhearted man, and his mentoring still means so much to me. His wife was one of the sweetest and most dedicated ladies I have ever met. We are still friends to this day.

Pastor Millard owned a large Buick Electra at the time, and he started taking me to various preaching conferences throughout the region. Several months later he took several of us to our first Sword of the Lord Conference. It was my first time to hear Dr. Jack Hyles and Dr. John R. Rice preach in person. I still remember the two sermons Brother Hyles preached: "There Is in This City a Man of God" and "What Do Ye More Than Others?"

Then one evening after church, my pastor came to me and urged me to go to the upcoming Pastors' School held yearly at the First Baptist Church of Hammond, Indiana. Two of my friends joined me, and we flew to Chicago. We knew this would be an unforgettable event.

I sat in awe as I saw the magnitude of First Baptist Church. During the opening ceremonies of Pastors' School, Dr. Hyles introduced each of the ministries of his church. Then the superintendent of the Pathfinder Department stepped out and introduced the ministry for the educable slow people of the area. She said, "I want to introduce you to the people of our Pathfinder Department. They prayed for you to have a safe trip to our Pastors' School." I was totally amazed at what she said and of course did not realize what was in my future with this Pathfinder Department.

After I returned from Pastors' School, I started visiting the county jail on Sunday afternoons. A friend of mine came to my room one night after my visit to the jail and told me that I should get some Bibles to give to the inmates. After he left, I prayed, "Dear Lord, please let me have some Bibles."

On Monday afternoon I went to the chaplain's office and asked him for some Bibles for my jail ministry. He gave me almost a dozen King James Gideon Bibles. He also sent me to a man who operated a small furniture store in Beaufort. When I arrived at the store, the owner gave me several boxes of Bibles. He then sent me to a person who owned a seafood business across the river. When I arrived, I met the owner's wife and said, "I was told that you might have some Bibles." As she was walking into the next room to get her husband, she commented, "You know, during breakfast my husband and I were talking about what we were going to do with all of the Bibles we have." Her husband took me to a small shed and opened the door. Inside the shed were over 300 Bibles! What an answer to prayer!

For some reason, on a Sunday night my pastor chose to preach Dr. Hyles' sermon, "Seven Steps to Success." At the invitation, I knew why. During the invitation, I surrendered to preach. After the service that night, Pastor Millard said, "God told me He was going to call someone to preach."

I began praying about what Christian college to attend. One night when I was in my room, I was reading the *Sword of the Lord*. On one of the pages was an advertisement for Hyles-Anderson College which stated, "Hyles-Anderson College is dead. It is dead to modernism, worldliness, and liberalism. Will you come and die with us?" That night the Lord touched my heart, and I decided to enroll in Hyles-Anderson College.

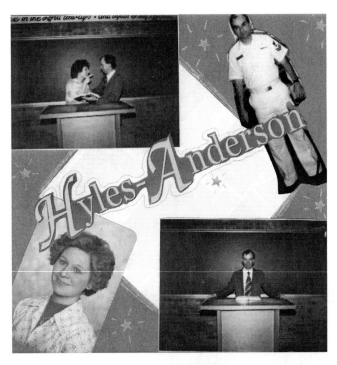

Love at First Sight:
Thanksgiving Day, November '79

3

Hyles-Anderson College

MY WIFE AND I met at Hyles-Anderson College during the Thanksgiving holiday. Several girls were sitting at the table, and someone, preferably a gentleman, needed to carve the turkey. One of them finally asked me to volunteer for the job. I was the only man sitting at the table with five or six ladies, and Rachelle was one of them. We laughed and clowned around a lot as I carved the turkey. I enjoyed a wonderful dinner with these young ladies.

Several days later I was studying in the library, and Rachelle also happened to be there. We chatted for a few minutes before she left. The following week we had our first chapel date. Chapel dates seemed to be everyone's first date for two reasons: it didn't cost anything to go to chapel, and everyone had to go to chapel. Since most of us did not have an abundance of money, chapel was a great place to date.

Because of our busy schedule with work and classes, most of our dates together were on the campus. We enjoyed playing board games together in the dining hall. Sorry and Uno became two of our favorite games. Rachelle and I laughed a lot when we played games. Everyone heard her laugh whenever she won.

In February we attended our first Valentine banquet together. Before we left for the banquet, we had our pictures taken together in the front lobby at the college. We boarded the bus to the Radisson Star Plaza in Merrillville for an enjoyable evening of dinner and a musical presentation.

At the end of our date that evening, Rachelle gave me a small windup toy in the shape of a heart. The words "My beating heart" were inscribed on it.

After six months of dating, Rachelle surprised me with a cassette tape recording of many of our friends' wishing us a happy six months' anniversary. I was really caught off guard at the number of faculty and staff who were wishing us a happy six months of dating. Rachelle even managed to get the chancellor of the college, Dr. Hyles, to include a short greeting on the tape.

Throughout our time of dating, I was busy taking a full load of classes and working full-time at the hospital as a phlebotomist. It was not unusual for me to put in a 16-hour day between classes, work, and study. Still, we managed to enjoy our time together.

During one of our dates, I told Rachelle that I loved her. However, she did not respond with the same reply. Instead she just sat there and looked at me with a smile on her face. I was really puzzled by her lack of response by the end of our date. For several weeks I kept telling her that I loved her and still received no response. I kept wondering what was wrong with the situation.

Finally on a Sunday morning in church, I found a big cookie from Rachelle sitting on the pew where we sat. When I opened the box, the words "I Love You too!" were written on the cookie.

The following June our friends, Rick Bartley and Iva King, were planning their wedding. Rick asked me to be his best man, and Rachelle was asked to be the guest book hostess. After the wedding was over, I met Rachelle at the college for another date.

At the time the college had an indoor miniature golf course on campus. In the middle of the golf course was a large porch swing. While we were sitting on the swing together, I asked Rachelle to marry me. I thought for sure she would immediately and happily respond "Yes!" But she just sat there with that same big smile she was wearing when I told her that I loved her.

I remember thinking, "Can't this woman make up her mind about anything?" Because she came from a broken home, Rachelle was very nervous about our future together and scheduled an appointment with the dean of women, Mrs. Marlene Evans, and one with her pastor, Dr. Jack Hyles. Two weeks later she said yes, she would marry me.

We scheduled our wedding for December 26, 1980. Our wedding cake was made from ingredients at the local grocery store for around $30. Someone gave Rachelle her wedding dress. Another lady took the wedding pictures and had them developed at K-Mart. Pastor Hyles performed our wedding ceremony in front of a hundred people. We spent our honeymoon taking trips to Chicago to visit different museums while we stayed at

Rachelle and her dad

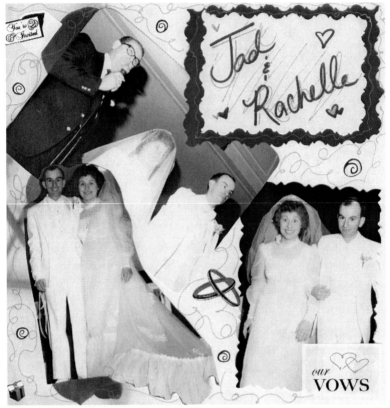

the Red Roof Inn in Merrillville. The total cost for our wedding was around $700. After the wedding, we knocked on Pastor Hyles' office door to give him a piece of our wedding cake. He opened the door and handed us our keepsake wedding license. When we opened the license later, we found $100 inside of it. We had a simple wedding, and we are still married after 30 years.

After our honeymoon, we moved into an unfinished basement apartment that was filled with pieces of used furniture which were given to us by Rachelle's father. Every night when we went to bed, we looked up and read "Owens Corning" on

the fiberglass insulation that was attached to the ceiling. The apartment had no closets, and we had to hang our clothes on a piece of pipe that was attached to the ceiling. The following summer we moved into a new apartment in Schererville. The apartment was so nice, we thought we were living in a luxury hotel!

Soon after we moved into our apartment, we became good friends with many of the other couples who attended college with us. Bryan and Camille Helm, who are now serving in Canada as missionaries, became two of our closest friends. Next to the parking lot of the apartment complex was a small

His Family

pond. Bryan and I both loved fishing; and in our spare time, we sneaked over to the pond to catch blue gill and catfish. We felt like two school-aged kids with our fishing poles. After an hour of fishing, the manager always came out on the balcony of his third-floor apartment and started yelling across the pond, "No fishing in the pond!" Usually after a week or two, we were back fishing in the pond. After many years, Bryan and I still laugh about our days of fun together at that pond.

Because I was in college, we always lived on a tight budget. I was still driving my little Toyota Corolla I had purchased while I was in the Navy. It had a four-speed stick shift trans-

mission, and Rachelle did not know how to drive it. The wife of one of my friends tried to teach her how to drive with a stick shift and did not succeed. One week later the starter went bad, and I did not have the money to replace it. The only way we were able to start the car was to push it and pop the clutch. I still remember one Sunday morning we were dressed for church, and it started raining. Rachelle was wearing her Sunday best when she held her opened umbrella with one hand and started pushing the car. I popped the clutch, and the car started. Luckily, she wasn't too wet when we arrived at our destination—church!

Above (front row): Jack Terrebonne, my wife and me, Juanita
Terrebonne, my grandmother, Rebecca Leboeuf
standing (left to right): my grandfather, Charles Leboeuf, Sr.
my sisters, Jacqueline, Glynis with her husband, R. J.
Duplanits, and Robin Terrebonne
Below: The bride's dad and sister Starr

*Above: The Terrebonnes with Pastor and Mrs. Den Karrow
and Brother and Mrs. Wally Davis
Below: with best man, Rick Bartley*

4

PAUL

IN OCTOBER OF 1982 I drew a blood sample from Rachelle at our apartment and took it to the laboratory where I worked. We had talked about the idea of having a baby, and it seemed as though she might be expecting. Several weeks earlier, I had gone out to the lake on our college campus and prayed, "Dear Lord, if Rachelle wants to have a baby, then please give us a son." Later that evening I called her at home and said, "Congratulations, we are going to have a baby."

I called my parents to tell them the good news. Everyone was excited about the coming of our first child. Dad was quick to mention, "Remember, the first grandson gets the gun." This was the first time his gun had been mentioned in ten years.

We contacted her doctor and made our first appointment. After her examination, he set the due date for June 21, 1983. Rachelle was experiencing constant nausea. The smell of anything made her sick. Whenever I cooked breakfast, the smell of eggs made her run to the bathroom. Her doctor assured her that this was a good sign that her progesterone levels were high enough to maintain her pregnancy.

After her second visit, he scheduled an ultrasound to check on the well-being of our new baby. I was able to be in the room with her when the ultrasound technician was able to see our child with the scanner and detect a heartbeat.

Throughout this time of waiting, we remained undecided on what to name our coming baby. When I was growing up as a Catholic, I went through the sacrament of "holy confirmation." During our class preparation, my catechism teacher asked Mom what she wanted for my confirmation name. She stated, "I want him to be called Anthony."

For some reason, I blurted out, "No, Mom! I want to be called Paul." Mom consented, and I was called Paul when I received the confirmation sacrament.

For some reason, that name came to my mind again, and I said, "If we have a boy, let's name him Paul Michael." After much discussion, we were not able to decide on a name if the baby was a girl. As it turned out, the name *Paul Michael* means, "Little one sent from God."

During this time, Rachelle was caring for a handicapped young lady whose parents attended our church. She also did baby-sitting for two small boys. Both of these jobs kept her busy, and at the end of the day, Rachelle came home tired.

In her sixth month of pregnancy, we enrolled in Lamaze classes taught by a lady in our church. The class was filled with young couples expecting their first child, along with a few other people who were taking a refresher course for their second child. I thought, "This is a great way to have a baby! Rachelle goes through all the labor, and all I have to do is remind her to say, 'HeeHeeHee Hoo. Take a cleansing breath in through your nose and out through your mouth.' "

One night while we were watching television, Rachelle started having severe abdominal pain. I was worried that she was going into premature labor and rushed her to the hospital. When we arrived at the hospital, the nurses started an IV in her hand and attached her to a fetal monitor. The doctor then ordered an ultrasound and an abdominal x-ray. After an hour the doctor returned and told us that she was having problems with her gall bladder. Rachelle was given some medicine to calm her gall bladder and admitted to the hospital for observation that night. The following day she was sent home and put on a low-fat diet.

It was 10:30 at night when Rachelle called the hospital to inform me that it was time to have the baby. I rushed home and found her curling her hair and putting on her makeup.

"What are you doing?" I anxiously asked.

"I want to look nice before I go to the hospital," she replied as she continued to work on her makeup.

"Aren't you are in labor with this baby?" I questioned. "Why do you want to look nice?"

"We are not going to the hospital until I look nice," she flatly maintained. "Please get my suitcase out of the closet while I curl my hair," she replied. Then it was time do her fingernails. An hour later we arrived at the hospital, and yes, Rachelle looked nice.

The rest of the evening, Rachelle did not experience many strong contractions. However, by the middle of the next morning, her contractions started getting stronger. At lunch time I decided to go to the cafeteria for a bite to eat and told Rachelle my plan. Rachelle looked at me and stated, "If I have to sit here and go through all of these labor pains, you're not going anywhere!" One of the nurses on duty was kind enough to send for a lunch tray for me to eat in the room with Rachelle.

Everything we learned in Lamaze classes fell into place. All of the lessons we took together gave me the confidence I needed to coach Rachelle during the birth of our first child. The fetal heart monitor showed the baby's heart rate was normal.

At five o'clock that afternoon, I changed into some surgical scrubs while the nurses prepared Rachelle for the delivery. The atmosphere in the delivery room was tense. I hugged Rachelle and helped her with her breathing as she began to push. At 5:57 p.m. the doctor looked up and said, "Congratulations! You have a baby boy." We kissed each other and said, "Yes! Paul gets the gun!" One of the nurses gave us a puzzled look about our comment. Several minutes later we were holding our newborn son, Paul Michael Terrebonne.

The nurses took him to the nursery for a bath and physi-

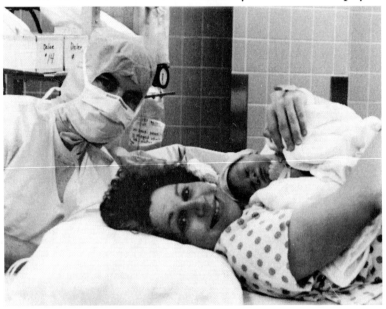

The proud parents of Paul

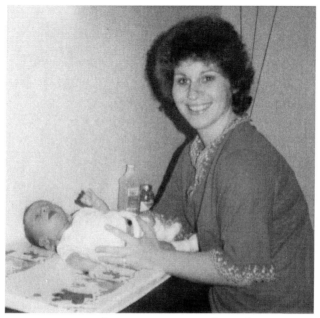

Brand-new mommy with Paul

cal exam then called the pediatrician. Paul was having a difficult time breathing and was put on oxygen. His white blood cell count was high, but his chest x-rays were normal. We prayed for God to watch over our son. We were very nervous since everything indicated that he was normal and healthy when he was born. His Apgar scores were 8/10.

Rachelle had another gall bladder attack the following day.

Grandma Dunkelberger and Paul

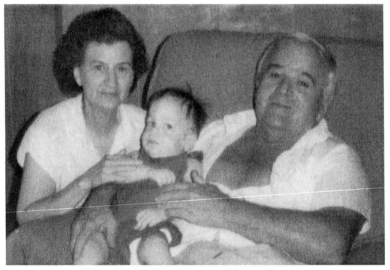

Paul's proud grandparents, Jack and Juanita Terrebonne

The doctors agreed that it was time for her to have surgery. She still teases me about how casually the doctor and I talked about her situation. She says we acted as though we were talking about the weather the whole time she was agonizing in pain.

Mom volunteered to help us with Paul while Rachelle recovered from surgery. Her help was a blessing to all of us. Dad was thrilled to have a new grandson. Several days later he went back to Louisiana.

Paul brought a lot of changes to our lives. Bath time, diaper changes, and 2:00 a.m. feedings became a regular part of our life. Rachelle adjusted well in her new role as a mother. She was very good at getting up for the feedings. As a matter of fact, she did all of the 2:00 a.m. feedings.

Several weeks later Paul had his first checkup with the

doctor. He received his first shots, and the doctor gave him a clean bill of health. Still, Rachelle sensed something different about Paul. "Jad, something is wrong with Paul. His eyes don't focus on me. They are not centered, and he keeps looking to the right."

One of our neighbors had a baby about the same time that Paul was born. Their son was doing things that Paul did not seem capable of doing. Rachelle kept insisting that Paul was not playing like the other children and that his problems were not normal for a baby his age. He constantly arched his back and was agitated before he went to sleep.

We discussed these problems with our pediatrician. He thought that Paul's eye muscles might be weak and with time he might grow out of it. The doctor was cautious but still optimistic.

I was in denial. "How can anything be wrong with Paul? Children develop differently," I rationalized. "It is not right to compare him to the other kids. He will grow out of it. Rachelle is a typical mother. She has nothing to worry about. I am his father, and everything is going to be fine. I have dreams about our future together."

Because the problems with Paul's eyes did not improve, we made an appointment with an ophthalmologist. Paul's pupils were dilated, and the doctor began to examine his eyes. Everything about Paul's eye exam appeared normal. After the doctor finished the exam, he scheduled an appointment for a pediatric ophthalmologist in Chicago.

We arrived in Chicago, hoping to find some answers to Paul's problems. We answered the usual questions about his development and behavior. The doctor performed a visual evoked response test on Paul, and the results were normal. She was beginning to believe that our son had neurological problems.

At fifteen months old, Paul had failed to reach six out of the nine developmental milestones for a child his age. Our pediatrician said, "I want you to know that Paul will be developmentally delayed all of his life. I am ordering a CT scan of his brain and an EEG. He needs to be enrolled into an early intervention program." His words shattered every dream I had for Paul.

I was forced to accept that Paul was going to be handicapped all of his life. When I arrived home, I laid him on the floor and prayed, "Dear Lord, You have a purpose for Paul's problems. Please make his life a miracle for Your glory."

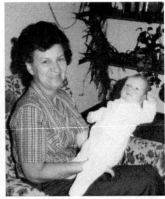

*Left: Rachelle, her mom,
and brother Craig
Above: Grandma
Terrebonne with Paul*

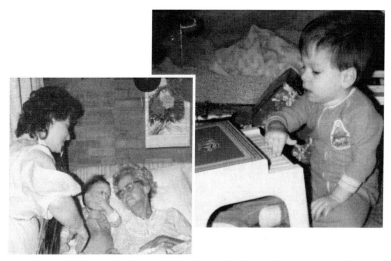

Above left: Rachelle and Paul with Coystal Mattie Hyles,
the mother of Dr. Jack Hyles
Above right: Paul with his piano
Below: Grandpa Terrebonne with Paul

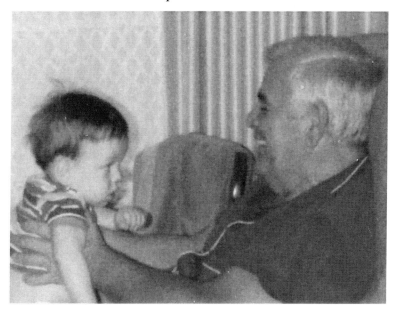

*Four generations: My grandmother, mother, and me
with Paul*

5

A Diagnosis

PAUL WAS SLEEPING on the table of the CAT scanner while the technician typed the commands into the computer. The table moved Paul into the scanner. Both Rachelle and I were concerned about what was happening with Paul. I was allowed to read the radiologist report. "Paul has a severe congenital cerebral malformation consisting in part to the partial agenesis of the corpus callosum and cerebellar hypoplasia." The scan also revealed that one side of his brain was smaller than the other.

The corpus callosum is a bundle of nerve fibers that connects the right and left side of the brain. It is responsible for almost all of the communication between the two hemispheres of the brain. Each part of the brain processes information from the five senses. This information is then transmitted to the other parts of the brain via this corpus callosum.

Since it did not develop properly in Paul's brain, the corpus callosum did not effectively transmit information between the left and right side of his brain. In some ways Paul behaved as though he had two separate brains. This explained why he had a gaze preference to the left side of his body.

Each new development about Paul raised more questions about his future.

- Did this diagnosis explain his bizarre behavior?

- Will he get better?
- Is this why he can't talk?
- Why is this happening to us?
- Is God angry at us?

God was definitely taking us on a different journey from the one we had planned. The questions lingered in our minds.

But God did not abandon us. As we took each step forward, He was always faithful in providing for our needs. The Lord said in Hebrews 13:5, "...*I will never leave thee, nor forsake thee.*"

Paul was enrolled in an accelerated program for developmentally delayed children. A physical therapist evaluated his ability to walk, climb stairs, and sit in different positions without help. An occupational therapist evaluated his ability to pick up objects and perform other detailed tasks using both of his hands. The speech therapist then tested his ability to say words and make various sounds. He received a hearing test and a complete physical examination by a doctor.

After all of the testing was done, we met with one of the social workers. He told us that Paul had cerebral palsy. Giving

Paul this diagnosis meant he could qualify to receive financial aid from the various local and state agencies. Based on our income, he was also qualified for supplemental security income from the Social Security Administration. Eventually, Paul was able to qualify for Indiana Medicaid.

I called the office of the agency involved and made an appointment to enroll Paul in the Crippled Children's program. I brought copies of my tax returns, bank accounts, and check stubs along with Paul's birth certificate, social security number, and a letter from the doctor with Paul's diagnosis. After a few weeks, the application we made on Paul's behalf was approved.

Because the office was in a rough part of town (Gary, Indiana), I decided to look as rough and tough as I could. I wore a pair of old blue jeans, an old flannel shirt, an old golf corduroy cap, and a pair of sneakers. I didn't shave that morning, and I put on my old Navy utility jacket to conceal the Colt .38 special I tucked into the waistband of my trousers. Throughout the interview with the case worker, I wore my gold-rimmed sunglasses and chewed on a toothpick. Whenever I answered any of her questions, I tilted the chair back on two legs. I was happy when the interview was over because I felt very uncomfortable with my gun jammed into my waist.

We were unhappy with the amount of therapy Paul was receiving from one of the agencies. Generally, each session lasted only 15 minutes. On some days he did not get any therapy at all if someone called off work. We decided to look somewhere else for help and found a therapy center in Crown

Point, Indiana. After another evaluation, Paul started receiving one hour of speech therapy, one hour of occupational therapy, and two hours of physical therapy each week. Rachelle and I were very happy with the new therapist who was also physically disabled. She encouraged us to attend the therapy sessions and gave us a list of toys that would help Paul develop his physical and mental skills.

Paul with one of his therapists having therapy

I was holding Paul while I relived many of the fishing and hunting trips I had made with my father. The times we had spent together gave me a lot of wonderful memories. Jesus said in John 12:24, *"Verily, verily, I say unto you, Except a corn of wheat fall into the ground and die, it abideth alone: but if it die, it bringeth forth much fruit."* I knew that the Lord had a purpose for Paul's suffering, but I had to wonder why He had let my dreams die.

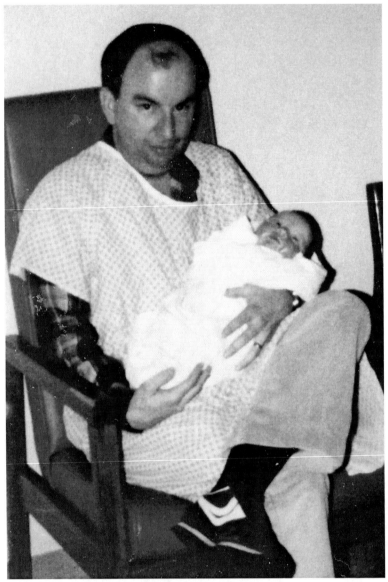

Daddy's Girl

6

AMY

O N OCTOBER 5, 1985, OUR daughter Amy was born. Rachelle and I were grateful to have a beautiful baby girl. In the early weeks of her pregnancy, Rachelle was bleeding, and we were nervous about losing the baby. However, after a few days the bleeding stopped, and the doctor ordered an ultrasound. We were happy to see that our baby was doing well.

Rachelle was three weeks past her due date, and the doctor was started getting concerned. He ordered a non-stress test to monitor the baby's heartbeat and was pleased to see that everything looked normal. He then started doing stress tests to monitor the fetal heart beat during labor. Everything continued to look good. Rachelle was just late in having this baby. The stress test did help stimulate Rachelle into going into labor, and our daughter was born.

When I held Amy in my arms for the first time, my heart was touched that I was the father of a beautiful daughter. She quickly became daddy's little girl.

We moved from our apartment into a three-bedroom house with a nice yard to accommodate our growing family. However, Paul did not adjust well to our new house. He spent a lot of time crying and throwing tantrums. He started biting and licking himself. After that, he became fixated with spinning the wheels of his toys. Rachelle and I were extremely puzzled by his behavior.

To supplement our income, I enlisted in the Navy Reserves. Because I was still working in the hospital laboratory, I was able to keep the same rank I held when I was released from active duty. Once a month we drilled at the local reserve center in Gary, Indiana.

One Saturday Rachelle called the reserve center because Paul was having a seizure. She told me he was lying on the floor and shaking violently. I told Rachelle to call "911" and that I would meet her at the emergency room. When the ambulance arrived, the lady next door volunteered to take

Mommy's Girl

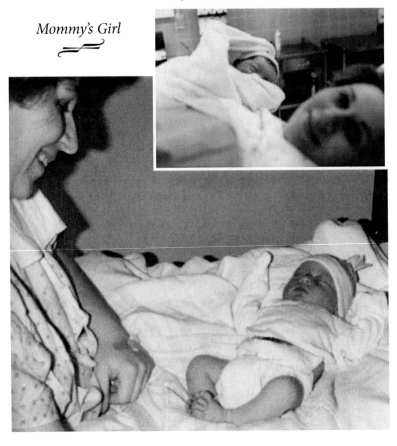

care of Amy. Rachelle told me later that Amy was very frightened and clung to our neighbor.

When I arrived at the hospital, Paul's seizure was over. The attending physician gave him a dose of phenobarbital through an I.V. A few hours later Paul was released from the hospital and scheduled for a follow-up appointment with his pediatrician.

His doctor believed that Paul's seizure was a reaction to his recent episode of chicken pox. He told us to monitor Paul carefully for any further signs of seizures. But after one month, Paul had another seizure that lasted for more than 15 minutes. I carried him to his room, placed him on his stomach, and turned his head to one side. I carefully monitored his pulse and respirations. When the seizure was over, Paul's right arm was paralyzed for 45 minutes.

With this event, the doctor then scheduled an EEG for Paul. Once the electrodes were attached to his scalp, the technician turned down the lights and started the EEG. Rachelle and I both watched as the pins began to trace the electrical impulses from Paul's brain on the moving sheets of paper. The results of the test were as follows:

> The sleep architecture is abnormal and suggests a diffuse encephalopathy. Sharp waves appear to be present in an asymmetrical fashion suggesting the presence of cortical irritability over the left posterior hemisphere. This could be associated with an epileptic diathesis. This is a significantly abnormal EEG.

The doctor's diagnosis was epilepsy. He prescribed Tegretol three times a day to control the seizures. Paul also had to have regular blood tests to monitor the levels of Tegretol. Over the course of time, he started receiving an adult dosage of medication to keep his seizures under control.

Throughout those difficult days, I kept pondering the reason for Paul's suffering. I was always asking God to show me the purpose for my son's life. One day at work God spoke to my heart through John 9:1-5: *"And as Jesus passed by, he saw a man which was blind from his birth. And his disciples asked him, saying, Master, who did sin, this man, or his parents, that he was born blind? Jesus answered, Neither hath this man sinned, nor his parents: but that the works of God should be manifest in him. I must work the works of him that sent me, while it is day: the night cometh, when no man can work. As long as I am in the world, I am the light of the world."* When I arrived home from work, I showed these verses to Rachelle.

"How can these verses apply to Paul?" she asked.

"I don't know, but I am going to claim them for Paul's life." I replied.

As I read these verses, I prayed, "Dear Lord, if You can manifest Your works in this blind man, please manifest Your works in our son. Please don't let Paul suffer in vain." Slowly God began to replace my broken dreams with a vision of what He can do in the life of an afflicted child.

The question asked to Jesus by the disciples, *"Master, who did sin, this man, or his parents, that he was born blind?"* reveals the confusion and ignorance of both the disciples and the others who knew this blind man. The people of that time period believed in various erroneous teachings that led to the confusion of this blind man's situation.

Some believed that he was suffering because of some sin

that his parents had committed. Others believed that this blind man was suffering from sin that he had committed in a previous life or that he had sinned while he was still in his mother's womb. Even his poverty was considered to be punishment from God. All of these beliefs led to a constant state of fear and confusion in the life of this man and his parents.

Notice how truth always sets the record straight during difficult trials. Jesus answered, *"Neither hath this man sinned, nor his parents: but that the works of God should be manifest in him."* This poor family suffered many years of fear, confusion, and guilt because their son was born blind. Yet they were not abandoned by God.

My first lesson to learn in our situation was that God was not angry at my wife or me. Rather, He had a special work that He was going to manifest in the life of our son. These verses have been the anchor for our family for the last 27 years. God would use these verses to lead us on an incredible journey that would test the very core of our faith in Him.

Paul and Amy

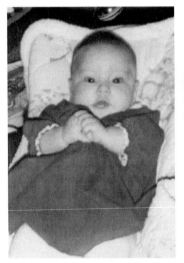

Upper left: Amy's First Christmas

Upper right and center: Grandma Terrebonne with Amy

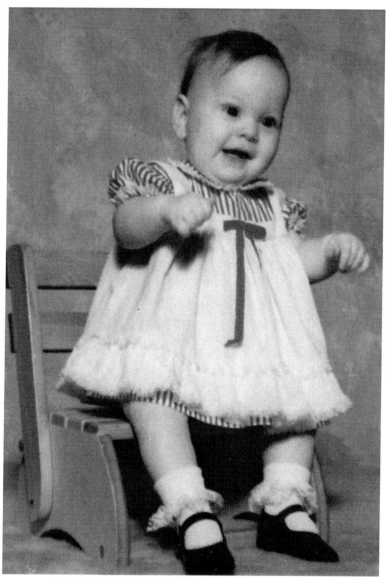

Amy at six months old

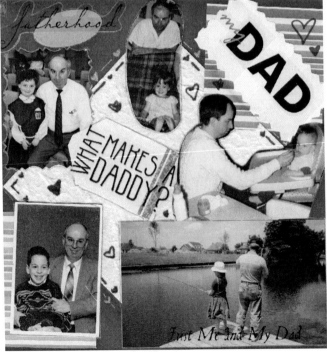

7

A Move

THE SCHOOL DISTRICT in which we lived did not have classes for handicapped children. We had to use the county co-op school for special needs children. To make matters worse, the bus ride was over an hour each way, and the classes only lasted half a day. Since the co-op had to accommodate several school districts, actual class time was very limited. We decided to move to Merrillville in order to enroll Paul in a better program.

Our real estate agent located a house that he felt might meet our needs. Even though the house needed a lot of repairs, we decided to put a bid on it. Fortunately, the house was owned by another real estate company. In their eagerness to sell the house, they agreed to pay all of our closing costs, including the first year of insurance, taxes, and the first house payment. God gave us another miracle on Paul's behalf.

As usual, Paul did not respond well to the new move, and his behavior continued to deteriorate. When he was not spinning the wheels on his toys, he was constantly turning the water faucets on and off. The lights in our house were constantly going on and off because he would not stop playing with the light switches. When he wasn't playing with the light switches, he was opening the refrigerator door and slamming it shut. Eventually all of the light switches had to be covered with tape. With time, Paul learned how to peel the tape off of the light switches, and he started flipping them on and off again. We couldn't take him shopping because he was constantly throwing tantrums. Little by little we became hermits in our own house.

One afternoon Rachelle noticed a blank look on Paul's face while he sat on the floor. His lower lip was sagging as he drooled out of the corner of his mouth. After each one of these spells, Paul became very agitated and started crying. His doctor said that Paul was having petit mal seizures.

Finally his doctor said, "I know when it is time to punt. We've done all that we can. It's time for you to go to the University of Chicago. I'll make some phone calls and get back with you."

The next day we received a call from the University of Chicago. The doctor sensed the tension in Rachelle's voice while she interviewed her about Paul's problems. When the interview was over, she agreed to schedule an appointment to see Paul.

When we arrived for our appointment, the doctor encouraged us to let Paul wander around the office. As we continued to discuss his medical history, Paul kept playing with the water faucets and light switches. After the interview, she left the office to contact my insurance company.

Upon her return she looked at both of us and said, "Both of you are exhausted. You need a break, and Paul needs our help. Your insurance agreed to cover the cost, provided he is admitted through the emergency room. In the meantime, I will assemble a team of doctors and see you in the emergency room next week."

The following week we met with the doctors at the emergency room as planned. Upon their examination, Paul was admitted to the hospital. One of the doctors on the team was the renowned Dr. Peter Huttenlocher, who was well-known for his research in pediatric neurology. To his fellow doctors he was respected as the "godfather of pediatric neurology." The next morning Dr. Huttenlocher examined Paul and talked with us about his plans for Paul during the upcoming weeks. Paul was to be transferred to the Chicago Lakeshore Hospital for a complete neuropsychological workup.

We arrived with Paul at Chicago Lakeshore Hospital after lunch with a list of all the tests he was to have done. The doctor who greeted us told us that Paul would be hospitalized for at least six weeks. She assured us that Paul was in good hands and advised us to get some rest.

The next day I went to my supervisor's office to tell her about what was happening with Paul. Somehow we met each other in front of the elevators. Before I could say anything, my supervisor looked at me and said, "You need some time off for your son, don't you?" As soon as we got off of the elevator, she turned and said, "Take all the time off you need. Call me when you are ready to come back to work."

I then called my parents, and they agreed to take care of Amy for us. The next day I was on a plane to New Orleans with Amy. When I arrived in Louisiana, one of my sisters met me at the airport and drove us back to Houma. I spent a couple of nights with my parents to allow Amy to get adjusted to her new surroundings and flew back to Chicago.

When I arrived back at the hospital, Rachelle and I met with one of the pediatric psychiatrists assigned to Paul. He conducted a lengthy interview about our family history and Paul's problems. He seemed to be very kind and probed us with detailed questions about our past. After the interview, he explained what was going to happen over the next several weeks. We were also told not to return to the hospital for one week. He wanted to evaluate Paul's behavior without our being there. He encouraged us to use this time to get some rest and to enjoy the Chicago area.

Rachelle and I agreed to follow his advice and visited several of the museums in the area. We took a pleasant walk along the lakefront and enjoyed a picnic in the park. This time of rest renewed our spirits for the long days ahead.

At the end of the week, we met with one of the doctors who was caring for Paul. She gave us the following assessment: "Paul is a severely delayed child in all areas of function. He is

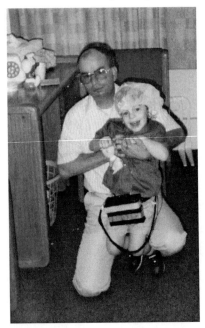

functioning at the level of a seven-month-old infant. His language production and comprehension are minimal. He appeared to show autistic-like behaviors. Paul also showed difficulty in processing visual information on both sides of space, and crossing the visual midline. These observations are consistent with agenesis of the corpus callosum."

Another doctor who had also examined Paul

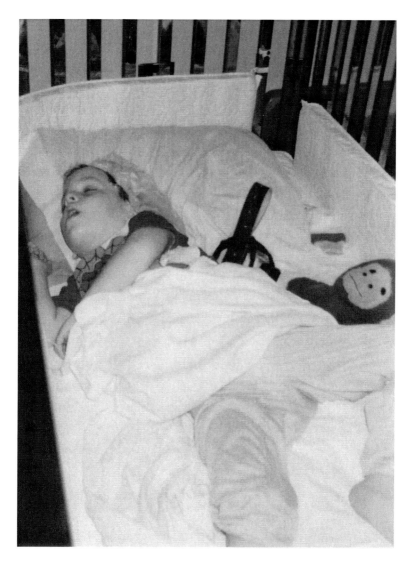

Left: Holding Paul during his 24-hour EEG

Above: Paul resting at the Chicago Lakeshore Hospital

concluded that he had additional unseen neurological problems.

Paul's 24-hour EEG showed he was still having problems with his seizures. This discovery explained the vacant stares and drooling. His Tegretol levels were gradually increased to two hundred milligrams three times a day.

We also attended family management classes on how to deal with special needs children. One of the doctors made a video of our playing together with a box of toys. I decided to ham it up while we played with toy dinosaurs. Another afternoon we attended an outdoor art therapy session. We were given a box of crayons and some paper to draw pictures of our family and explain our difficulties to the rest of the class.

During one of our visits, Paul's doctor gave us some general ideas about handling Paul. Since Paul was so developmentally delayed, he suggested using simple one-word commands. He stated bluntly, "You will need to talk to Paul as though he were an animal. Paul eat, Paul drink etc." He also instructed us to always look Paul straight in the eye whenever we spoke to him. His final statement to us that day shook me to the core. "One of these days you will have to institutionalize your son," he flatly stated. He made me realize, for the first time, that at some time in the future Paul would need more help than we were capable of giving him.

At the end of six weeks, Paul was released from the hospital. I finished signing all of the discharge papers when the clerk gave me a copy of the hospital bill. The total came to over $46,000. My insurance agreed to pay all but $9,000. I almost laughed when he asked me if I wanted to write a check for that amount. He allowed me to fill out a financial disclosure form detailing my income and monthly expenses. Paul's doctor agreed to talk to the hospital administration on our behalf while they reviewed our financial statements. The administration agreed to reduce our bill to the amount the insurance had paid. God is in the miracle-working business!

God used this period in our life to give me a different outlook on Paul's situation. The issue was no longer about my broken dreams; rather, my focus turned to the suffering of our entire family. I had a handicapped son, but Amy had to deal with a handicapped brother.

Rachelle bore the heartache of having an afflicted son and couldn't take Paul out to play with the other children in the neighborhood. I did not have the normal father and son relationship that I wanted. But Amy lost a normal brother-sister relationship, and Rachelle lost a normal mother-son relationship.

Daniel 3:23 states, *"And these three men, Shadrach, Meshach, and Abed-nego, fell down bound into the midst of the burning fiery furnace."* Notice how God mentions each one of these men by name. It is important to know that it was not just a group of men who were thrown into that hot furnace that day; rather, three individual people had to face the fire. Each one of them had a different measure of faith and fears, but it is also important to know that they fell into the fire collectively.

In verse 24 Nebuchadnezzar states, *"Did not we cast three men bound into the midst of the fire?"* Whenever trials come into a family, all the members of the family all suffer both individually and collectively. The Bible says in I Corinthians 12:26, *"And whether one member suffer, all the members suffer with it...."*

Next they all walked together. Daniel 3:25, *"He answered and said, Lo, I see four men loose, walking in the midst of the fire, and they have no hurt; and the form of the fourth is like the Son of God."* These three men not only suffered together, but they walked together. Notice that there is no mention of any one of them blaming each other for their predicament. All three of them fell into a situation that was beyond their control, and they got up and continued walking together. It is very important for families to stick together during times of trials and temptations.

Notice in verse 25 how Shadrach, Meshach, and Abednego were now walking unfettered in the midst of the fire. They were cast into the fire bound, and Nebuchadnezzar could see that they were now free. All three of them were still in the fire, but they were walking freely with a fourth person. God always uses trials to reveal His presence. What the king used in an effort to destroy these three men, God used to set them free. What the fire could not do in destroying them, it did in freeing them because Jesus was with them in the midst of the fire.

8

"God, I Hate This!"

"Even to day is my complaint bitter: my stroke is heavier than my groaning." (Job 23:2)

"**G**OD, I DO not like having a disabled son...." Yes, you read my words right. I hate this. I am just being honest. I am only human and completely selfish. I am sick and tired of dealing with this problem.

"God, what in the world is going on here? I am not one bit interested in Romans 8:28! It's all going to work out for good? Yeah, right. I just want to quit and throw in the towel."

"Hey God, I want to take Paul fishing if You don't mind. We want to play catch in the backyard. Why did You do this to me? Can't You see I hate this? Phooey on being conformed to Your will. I want things my way. I was supposed to take him duck hunting. Remember the gun Dad promised him?

"I hate epilepsy, God. This is not what I had in mind. Do You remember the first time Paul had a seizure? He fell on the floor and started flopping around like a fish. My wife called '911,' and we were scared to death. God, that wasn't funny. I am just being honest with You. The technician who did Paul's EEG glued a bunch of red, white, and blue wires to his head. When she was finished, Paul looked like he was from outer space.

"Autism stinks! God, can't You see how Paul is playing with the faucets and light switches? The whole house is covered with duct tape. Look how he spins the wheels on his toys. This kid is driving me nuts!

"Paul's brain damage is the absolute pits. The doctors say that the left side of his brain is not connected to the right side of his brain. It's not my fault he is running around the house as though he has two brains in his head.

"And God, I am tired of his tantrums. Every time he gets upset, he falls down on the floor and plays spaghetti legs. Trying to get him off the floor is like playing with a wet noodle. God, it's Your turn to come down here and deal with this.

"Last month I had to go to the welfare office. Did You hear all of those embarrassing questions I had to answer? All that paper work drove me nuts. Once every three months the social worker comes to the house dressed like a spy.

"God, I am fed up with having to drive to Silvercrest once a month. The nice video the social worker showed us was a bunch of baloney. Never mind that it is over 250 miles away. Taking Paul there is like dropping him off at the county jail. Once a month the 'guards' call to tell us that Paul is sick. And besides that, their yellow Jell-O tastes bad.

"These quarterly reviews and annual case conferences are completely boring. I'd rather watch paint dry on the wall. Paul's teachers talk about his progress and their goals for his future. Then they give us a copy of his Individual Education Plan. It sounds so sweet, I want to vomit.

"We had to admit Paul to the University of Chicago Hospital. The doctors ran dozens of tests on him. They gave us these amazing answers about Paul. Then one of them said,

'There's not much we can do.' Lord, what was that all about? "Paul was anointed with oil, and he is still autistic. Why didn't You answer our prayers? What is the problem here?"

The hardest part of this entire ordeal is being honest with God about my thoughts and feelings concerning Paul. Bearing my soul to the Lord and allowing myself to open up to Him has not been easy. I remember going into Paul's room one time with my notebook full of prayer lists. In frustration I threw it across the bed and said, "God, You and I need to have a talk." It was the beginning of a whole new attitude toward my prayer time with God. Little by little, I started telling God whatever was on my mind. I quit trying to "hide" my feelings from Him.

Through the years I've learned that if I pour out my heart before God, I am less likely to take out my frustrations on my family. I am sad to admit that taking out my frustrations on my family is a mistake I've made too many times.

Psalm 142:2 says, *"I poured out my complaint before him; I shewed before him my trouble."* The word *poured* means "to spill and gush out intensely." It also means "to vomit with lots of noise and intensity." God is essentially saying, "Come to Me and vomit it all out before Me."

Psalm 42:4, *"When I remember these things, I **pour** out my soul in me."*

Psalm 62:8, *"Trust in him at all times; ye people, **pour** out your heart before him: God is a refuge for us. Selah."*

Just like a mom puts a diaper on her shoulder when burping her baby, God is big enough for us to burp out all of our problems before Him.

SOME OBSERVATIONS

1. **God knows your thoughts.** I Chronicles 28:9 says, "...*for the* LORD *searcheth all hearts, and understandeth all the imaginations of the thoughts*...." Psalm 94:11 says, "*The* LORD *knoweth the thoughts of man*...." If God knows and understands my thoughts, then why try to hide them from Him? If I try to hide my thoughts from Him, then I am opening the door to bitterness and frustration.

2. **Be totally honest with God about everything.** Hebrews 4:16, "*Let us therefore come boldly unto the throne of grace, that we may obtain mercy, and find grace to help in time of need.*" One of the meanings of *boldly* is "to be totally frank and honest." When was the last time you were completely honest about how you felt about your problems or sorrows? It is nice to know that I don't have to pretend to be a good Christian before God when I discuss my problems; I just need to be honest.

3. **Cry out to God.** Psalm 28:1, 2, "*Unto thee will I cry, O* LORD *my rock; be not silent to me: lest, if thou be silent to me, I become like them that go down into the pit. Hear the voice of my supplications, when I cry unto thee, when I lift up my hands toward thy holy oracle.*" The word *cry* in the first verse means "to walk up to someone and address them abruptly." The word *cry* in the second verse means "to cry out with noise in order to be rescued from trouble." A person who is drowning cries out and lifts up his hand for someone to rescue him. God wants us to come quickly to Him and to cry out to Him to deliver us from our troubles.

4. Weep before God. Psalm 39:12a, *"Hear my prayer, O LORD, and give ear unto my cry; hold not thy peace at my tears."*

Psalm 56:8, *"Thou tellest my wanderings: put thou my tears into thy bottle: are they not in thy book?"* If we are honest with our thoughts toward God, then we can be honest about our tears. It is good to shed our tears before God. He is a wonderful and compassionate Saviour Who wants to see your tears.

SILVERCREST

IN LESS THAN two years, Paul was out of control again. We did everything we were told to do by every doctor and specialist we saw. It seemed as though we were always taking one step forward and two steps backward. His autistic behavior became worse. As he grew older, he became stronger and was even able to pull the handle off of the refrigerator door. We were at our wits end when Rachelle came down the hall one afternoon and said, "I can't take this anymore; something needs to be done with Paul." Immediately I heard the doctor's words, "You know Paul is going to have to be institutionalized one day," echoing in my mind.

Norma, our social worker, did not know of any places that could take Paul. She agreed to look into the matter and found a place called Silvercrest Development Center in New Albany, Indiana.

We contacted the center and made an appointment for them to visit Paul in our house. While the case workers observed his behavior, Rachelle and I watched a video about the facilities. After the interview, we had another stack of forms to fill out. We also needed a letter from Paul's doctor outlining his problems.

Before we made any final decisions, we scheduled an appointment with Pastor Hyles. On the day of our appointment, we took Paul and Amy with us. Paul started misbehaving immediately. When he wasn't playing with the items on Dr. Hyles' desk, he was turning the lights on and off. Then he ran into Pastor Hyles' bathroom. When our pastor realized that Paul was behaving in this manner all of the time, he approved our decision to send him to Silvercrest.

In the early spring, we drove to New Albany to have Paul evaluated for his admission to Silvercrest. When we arrived, we were greeted by several of the social workers and therapists. Every person we met expressed a personal interest in helping Paul.

During his evaluation, Rachelle and I took Amy for a walk around the campus, which was surrounded by beautiful oak trees. While Amy played on the swings, Rachelle and I discussed Paul's future. We hated to leave Paul in New Albany, 250 miles from home. Paul was out of control, and nothing we were doing at home was working. As difficult as it was, we decided to follow through with our pastor's advice.

We were allowed to spend the night in one of the duplexes on the campus. The room was sparsely furnished, but the price was right—free. Since the kids were little, we pushed the three beds together and had a big pajama party.

The following afternoon, everyone was finished with evaluating Paul. We would receive a letter announcing the decision on whether or not to accept Paul into Silvercrest. The letter did come in the mail, and Paul was accepted into their program.

On May 8, we packed Paul's belonging and drove back to New Albany. We arrived in time for lunch and were allowed to eat in the cafeteria. As we carried our green pastel trays through the line, the workers took turns plopping round scoops of food onto our trays. We also got a piece of mystery meat. The last server gave us a square piece of yellow cake. Our plastic-ribbed glasses were filled with warm grape Kool-Aid. Our mood was as dreary as the food.

Silvercrest: Rachelle, Paul, and Amy

After lunch we unpacked Paul's clothes and placed them in the dresser next to his bed. He would be sharing a room with six other children. We hung a mobile of red, blue, and yellow cloth balloons above his bed. At that point reality set in: Paul was not coming home.

After we finished unpacking, I took Paul outside for a short walk. I wept openly, knowing that Paul might never live in our home again. Rachelle and Amy followed as we all huddled around him to say goodbye. It was one of the saddest days of our lives. We continued to cry as we hugged Paul for the last time before we drove back home.

When we arrived home that afternoon, we peeled the tape from the light switches and refrigerator door. This little event marked another milestone in our journey to help Paul.

Silvercrest: celebrating Paul's birthday

10

"Which Way Do We Go?"

Dad had his flashlight focused on the compass while Norman was looking into the dense fog. We were on another duck hunting trip, and the visibility was nearly zero as we crossed Lake Decad in Norman's boat. The only directions we had to the hunting camp were the coordinates given to us by the owner.

The day before our trip, the men looked over one of Dad's many navigational maps. Norman pointed to the location of the hunting camp, and Dad scribbled down the coordinates.

Norman was "Mr. Yakety-Yak" while he was driving the boat. Dad was the quiet one who never took his eyes of the compass. His only response to Norman's endless questions about our direction was, "A little to the right, Norman." Then a few minutes later, "A little to the left, Norman. Hold your course right there." I decided to look over Dad's shoulder at the compass rather than at the dense fog which surrounded us.

Out of nowhere a hapless coot landed in front of our boat. I loaded my gun and enjoyed the first kill of the day. We turned the boat around to pick it up out of the water and turned back in the direction we were headed.

Up until this time, our journey with Paul had been the same way as this duck hunting trip I had enjoyed as a boy.

Everything seemed to be in a fog. When we were not meeting with social workers, we were in the doctor's office discussing his medical problems. Then we were off to a physical therapy session. Paul's life at this point was a constant litany of testing, case management meetings, and therapy sessions with endless signatures on every form known to man. We had driven hundreds of miles and felt like mice running on little wire wheels going nowhere.

From recalling this duck hunting trip, I realized I had learned several valuable lessons.

1. Dad trusted his map and his compass. Dad did not let the dense fog and the confusion of Norman's endless chatter throw him off course. He never looked up and asked, "Well Norman, what do think we ought to do?" He just kept his eyes on the compass. Psalm 119:105 says, *"Thy word is a lamp unto my feet, and a light unto my path."* Just as the maps and compass provided us with safe directions, God's Word is the same way.

By now Dad had become a seasoned maritime navigator; he had learned to trust his books, his maps, and his compass. He didn't let the surrounding circumstances confuse him in regard to the direction he needed to take. God provides that same direction and wisdom when we are willing to trust His Word.

2. Dad didn't let the stray coot get him sidetracked. The fog was at its worst. To his credit, Dad picked up the coot, and we returned on our way. Imagine what our predicament might have been if Dad had said to Norman, "Why don't we just wander around in the fog and chase coots?" We would have never made it to the hunting camp and may well have ended up confused and lost or, worse yet, at the bottom of the lake.

Whenever we face trials, an endless number of "coots" seem to come our way to take us off course. There will always be people who are self-styled experts concerning your problem and will give you their opinion in the matter. These "coots" will always add confusion and fear to your sorrows. I Corinthians 14:33 says, *"For God is not the author of confusion...."* Over the years we have had our fair share of "coots" who have offered their opinions. Here is a sample of their comments:

- "What qualifications do these people have to care for your son?"
- "I have heard that Vitamin B12 can cure autism."
- "I have heard that childhood vaccines cause autism."
- "I am sorry to hear that Paul is demon possessed."
- "Now that you are retired, you can bring Paul home and take care of him yourself."
- "You should have Paul hypnotized." (my favorite)

I decided a long time ago to let these "coots" just keep on flying by.

3. Norman trusted Dad's wisdom. In spite of his constant chattering, Norman trusted Dad's wisdom and guidance in getting us across the lake. He knew full well that if we were going to make it safely across the lake, he had better be quiet long enough for Dad to keep him on course.

Proverbs 11:14 says, *"Where no counsel is, the people fall: but in the multitude of counsellors there is safety."*

Proverbs 24:6, *"For by wise counsel thou shalt make thy war: and in multitude of counsellors there is safety."*

Throughout the years, whenever my wife and I had to make major decisions about Paul, we went to see Dr. Hyles and now his successor, Pastor Jack Schaap, for counsel. We then sought out the top experts in those areas who knew how to help Paul best. Because we chose this path, I believe God has blessed us tremendously. And Paul has made progress beyond our expectations.

11

The Clouds Are Getting Darker

WHILE WE WERE still living in Highland, Indiana, Rachelle began having short lapses in her memory. She thought that it was from all of the stress with Paul and never mentioned it to me. One afternoon she decided to go grocery shopping. We discussed whether or not she should take Amy with her while I watched Paul. I decided that I would take care of both of them while she went shopping.

I was playing with the children in the backyard when a police officer pulled into our driveway an hour later. Rachelle was sitting inside the squad car. The officer explained that Rachelle had been in a car accident that rendered our car inoperable. He gave me a copy of the police report. Rachelle was making a right turn from a side street when she was hit by an oncoming car. Fortunately, no one was hurt. However, she was given a ticket for failure to yield the right of way.

A friend of mine took me to the gas station where the car had been towed. The car was a total wreck. I had just made the last payment on it, and the check had not yet cleared the bank. The main impact on the car was on the left rear passenger door next to Amy's car seat. I have no doubt that if Amy had been in the car that day, she would have been severely injured or even killed.

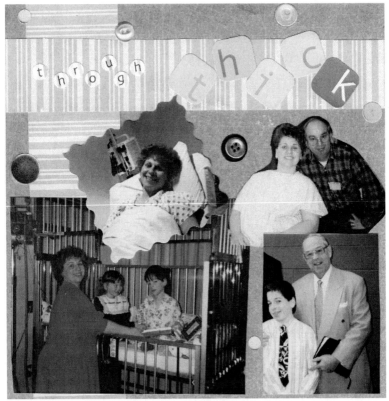

through thick

After we moved to Merrillville, Rachelle began having chronic headaches. Paul was already living at Silvercrest when we scheduled an appointment with a neurologist for Rachelle. During the course of her examination, Rachelle mentioned the problems with her memory lapses. The doctor checked all of her neurological reflexes and asked her several questions as to time of day, the names of our children, the President of the United States, etc. When he completed his exam, he ordered a CAT scan of her brain.

The radiologist report on her CAT scan indicated that she had a small growth deep inside her brain. A follow-up MRI

How I Give Up
My Broken
Dreams

by
Jad Terrebonne

Paul M. Terrebonne

revealed that the growth was indeed a brain tumor. The neurologist then referred us to a local neurosurgeon. The neurosurgeon did not appear overly alarmed about the matter, and he wanted to see her again in six months for another MRI in order to check whether or not the tumor was growing any larger.

Because we were not happy with his recommendations, Rachelle and I discussed our options and decided to call the University of Chicago Hospital right away. Two weeks later we were sitting outside a neurosurgeon's office with Rachelle holding her MRI scans.

The door opened, and Dr. Jean Mullen invited us into his office. He had short white hair and gray eyebrows that hung over his gold-rimmed glasses. He was a world-renowned physician and had pioneered many of today's modern neurosurgery techniques. To us, however, he would become the bearer of bad news.

He quickly pulled the MRI scans from the brown folder and put them up on the viewing box. With one slender finger pointing toward the scans, he looked at both of us, and I can still hear the words he calmly stated. "You have what appears to be a low-grade glioma. These tumors are usually slow growing and benign. However, they can become very malignant. You will need surgery to have it removed. I am additionally quite concerned about the location of your tumor. It is very deep and located between the memory and speech centers of your brain. Any complications from the surgery could wipe out your memory or take away your ability to speak. First I want to determine whether or not this tumor is malignant. If the tumor is benign, we can take our time and determine the course of action that needs to be taken before surgery. However, if the tumor is malignant, we have a major problem on our hands; and we will have to act quickly. First things first, I will order a PET scan of your brain. This will test how fast the tumor metabolizes an injection of radioactive glucose. This outcome will give us an idea of whether or not the tumor is malignant. If the radioactive uptake is high, it may well indicate a malignancy. If the uptake is slow, then chances are the tumor is benign. I also want to schedule a memory test to see if you have bilateral memory."

Rachelle and I were relieved to know that the radioactive

uptake from the tumor was slow. Rachelle's memory test showed that she was suffering from moderate memory loss and that she did have bilateral memory. All of the doctors were pleased with the results. Because we were nearing the Christmas season, Dr. Mullen scheduled Rachelle for surgery on January 31, 1990.

Throughout this time, Paul was constantly getting sick at Silvercrest. At least once a month, we received a call that he was running a fever and had strep throat. On one of our visits to Silvercrest, I found the cause of the problem. The workers were putting all of the children's toothbrushes in one cup. The bottom of the cup was filled with a brown liquid ooze. They were also sharing the same tube of toothpaste. I called the administrator and pitched a fit with him on the phone. He quickly agreed to resolve the matter.

On one of our trips to Silvercrest during the holidays, the social worker told us that we were allowed to be reimbursed for our travel expenses. By law, Paul's school in Merrillville had to pay us 50 cents a mile for every trip we made to see Paul. The school principal resisted our request until I read her my copy of what the law required. Our first check was for $750. When the school secretary handed me the check, she asked, "What are you going to do with all of that money?"

I looked at her and said, "Merry Christmas!"

We drove to Silvercrest during a snowstorm to bring Paul home for Christmas. When we arrived, no one bothered to tell us he was sick. He was running a high fever and was very weak. Upon our return home, we took Paul straight to the doctor. Paul was immediately sent to the hospital and admitted with severe dehydration the day before Christmas.

People from around the neighborhood and our church learned about Rachelle's brain tumor and Paul's stay in the hospital. Our next-door neighbor gave our names to one of the local charities. One evening there was a knock at the door. I opened the door to see several people from the town standing there with their arms filled with gifts, groceries, and an envelope with money in it. The next morning someone left a bag with seven new Barbie dolls in it for Amy. Our hearts were filled with gratitude for everyone's generosity.

After Christmas, we took Paul back to Silvercrest. It would be several months before we saw him again. January 31 was approaching like a hurricane brewing in the Gulf of Mexico. This time there were no evacuation routes; the eye of the storm was upon us.

12

Fear Not

THE DAY DR. Mullen told us that Rachelle had a brain tumor, my whole life flashed before my eyes. One night on my way to work, the Lord spoke to my heart and said, "Fear not." I knew a verse in the Bible mentioned these two words. After work the next morning, I found Isaiah 43:1, 2, *"But now thus saith the LORD that created thee O Jacob, and he that formed the, O Israel, Fear not: for I have redeemed thee, I have called thee by thy name; thou art mine. When thou passest through the waters, I will be with thee; and through the rivers, they shall not overflow thee: when thou walkest through the fire, thou shalt not be burned; neither shall the flame kindle upon thee."* Upon reading these verses, I realized that I had underlined them when I was reading my Bible one night while I was still in the Navy. God was saying to me, "When troubles come your way, don't forget Who saved you. I haven't forgotten who you are, and you still belong to Me."

The word *water* in verse two is the Hebrew word *mayim* which means "wasting water." In other words, *mayim* means "human waste or sewer water." God is saying that when it seems that life is flushing you down the toilet, He will be with you.

I remember a time when I was still living with my parents and our septic system started backing up. We couldn't flush the toilets, and all of the drains backed up. Dad dug a hole and found the septic tank cover. It was my job to get a stick and unplug the drain hole every day until the septic tank cleaners came to empty the tank. It was a nasty, thankless job.

Our lives at this point seemed to be going down the sewer. Paul was 250 miles away in New Albany. Rachelle was in Chicago getting ready for brain surgery. Yet God assured us that He had not abandoned us. I clung to these verses throughout the entire ordeal.

About two weeks before the surgery, Dr. Mullen ordered a three-dimensional MRI of Rachelle's brain. This test helped him to determine the best location to enter her brain to remove the tumor. On the morning of surgery, Dr. Johnny Colsten, an associate pastor from First Baptist Church of Hammond, Indiana, came to the hospital and prayed with us. We had a very real sense of God's presence during our time of prayer together.

At 7:30 a.m. I followed Rachelle as she was wheeled to surgery. We stopped outside of the doors to the operating room and hugged each other. So many questions went through my mind as she entered the operating room.

Once inside the operating room, Rachelle was prepared for surgery. One of the nurses started an I.V. in her hand. A surgery technician shaved a small portion of her scalp where the doctor needed to make the incision. Electrodes were attached to her chest to monitor her heartbeat. The atmosphere was quiet and professional.

Dr. Mullen entered the room and looked over the MRI scans. While he looked over the scans, the anesthesiologist administered the drugs that sedated Rachelle. The doctors wanted her to be partially awake in order to monitor her physical responses during the surgery. She was asked various questions in order to determine if any brain damage occurred during surgery.

Everyone was somber as Dr. Mullen used a scalpel to make the first incision across Rachelle's scalp line. The skin was spread apart and held in place with various tissue clamps while the surgical nurse sponged away the blood. When the bleeding was under control, a hole was drilled into her skull. Using the microscopic techniques he had pioneered, Dr. Mullen slowly and carefully made his way to the tumor. Once he reached the tumor, a small piece of it was removed and sent to the pathology lab for a biopsy. Rachelle's life was on the line.

The minutes turned into hours as I sat in the waiting room. Because of my work experience at the hospital, I was comfortable with my surroundings. However, I was still nervous about Rachelle and what the future held for us. I kept my Bible opened to Isaiah 43:1 throughout the time she was in surgery. As the day went by, the nurse kept me updated on the progress of Rachelle's surgery. She was very kind and encouraged me to go and have lunch. I agreed and went to the cafeteria for a quick bite to eat.

At 3:30 that afternoon, the nurse called me from the waiting room and led me to small private room. Within a few minutes, Dr. Mullen arrived. We shook hands and sat down together. He told me that the tumor was about the size of his thumb and fairly solid. To my relief it was not malignant. He explained that during the surgery, some swelling occurred and cut off the blood supply to part of her brain. As a result, she was partially paralyzed on the right side of her body. However, Dr. Mullen was confident that with intense therapy, she would regain most of her strength.

After our meeting, I went to the Neuro Intensive Care Unit to visit with my wife. Her eyelids were black and blue and almost swollen shut. She recognized me even though she was still heavily sedated. The nurse restricted my visit to 15 minutes. Then a little while later he came with a dinner tray and allowed me to feed Rachelle her dinner. His act of kindness made it possible for me to stay with her an additional half hour.

Along with being partially paralyzed, Rachelle suffered from aphasia, a condition that occurs when a person cannot match his words with his thoughts. As I write this chapter, I can remember our having many interesting conversations.

The day after surgery Rachelle started her therapy. At first the therapist came to her room. As she gained her strength, Rachelle was able to go downstairs to the physical therapy center.

Rachelle in therapy

While she was in the hospital, Rachelle's sister, Starr, flew in from California to help us. Starr was a beautician at the time, so she styled Rachelle's hair to cover up the sutures from the incision in her scalp. She also cared for Amy and helped with the cooking. Starr prepared some of the best Persian food I have ever eaten. What a blessing she was to us during our time of need!

After two weeks Rachelle was able to come home from the hospital. The following Sunday she surprised everyone and

Home after surgery with sister Starr and Amy

came to church. The members of our Sunday school class were stunned to see her. God was working in miraculous ways. Her faithfulness to church gave all of us a wonderful spiritual boost. That week Rachelle used her left hand to write a short note thanking Pastor Hyles and the rest of the church for their prayers.

Not only did the surgery affect her physically, but it affected her emotionally as well. On any given day she experienced severe mood swings. One moment she was extremely happy, and several hours later she was severely depressed and started crying. During her emotional downturns, she would start to talk about committing suicide. As a precaution, I removed my guns from the house and took them over to a friend of mine for safekeeping. One night I found Rachelle crying as she sat on the bed. She wept as she told me that she was unable to use her right hand. I held her hand and looked her squarely in the eye and said, "Don't you quit on me; you can make it. Now squeeze my hand!" Several seconds later her right hand closed slowly around mine. This moment of strength gave her the courage to keep going.

Several days a week she underwent intense physical, occupational, and speech therapy. Rachelle had to hold a pencil properly in her right hand and learn to write all over again. The therapist wrapped a long strand of putty around her fingers. She then had to stretch her fingers against the resistance of the putty and then squeeze it into a round ball. Once the putty was shaped into a round ball, she kneaded it into various shapes and had to pull it into taffy-like strands. She also had to work in the kitchen using various utensils. At the end of the day she was told to prepare our evening meals.

During speech therapy, Rachelle had to sit in front of a mirror and move various parts of her face. She also had to pronounce words using various facial expressions. During one of her sessions, someone asked her what day it was. She could not remember even though a calendar was on the wall next to where she was sitting. Rachelle was also taught how to eat without biting her tongue.

Physical therapy was just as rigorous. Rachelle had to ride a stationary bike, walk on a treadmill, and do an endless number of leg lifts with a physical therapist pushing down on her legs. Specific exercises were used to develop the strength of her feet and toes. She also had to take many walks.

As the months passed, Rachelle made tremendous strides in regaining her strength. Dr. Mullen also took her off of the phenobarbital since she was not having any seizures. During this time, both the doctor and the therapist advised Rachelle not to drive.

I was working the night shift at the time, and we had one car. While I was sleeping during the day, Rachelle sneaked out of the house and drove around the neighborhood. This went on for several weeks without my knowledge.

One afternoon she asked me to go with her for a drive around the neighborhood. I was understandably nervous yet excited about this giant step forward on her part. However, she was not content to stay in the neighborhood and took us out on Route 30. Within seconds we were going over 50 miles per hour in open traffic. I looked at her and yelled, "You are going to get us all killed!"

From that day on, Rachelle had the keys to the car.

Rachelle with Mrs. Beverly Hyles (two months after surgery)

13

WHAT ABOUT OUR MARRIAGE?

"Therefore shall a man leave his father and his mother, and shall cleave unto his wife: and they shall be one flesh." (Genesis 2:24)

"Therefore whosoever heareth these sayings of mine, and doeth them, I will liken him unto a wise man, which built his house upon a rock: And the rain descended, and the floods came, and the winds blew, and beat upon that house; and it fell not: for it was founded upon a rock." (Matthew 7:24)

WE EXCHANGED OUR wedding vows that December night among family and friends. The church auditorium was adorned with Christmas decorations, and music filled the atmosphere with love and romance. Our newly formed marriage was alive with hopes and dreams—not knowing all of what life would be sending our way.

Those wedding vows sound so nice in the right atmosphere. A couple promises to love and to cherish each other through the good and bad times, in sickness and health, for richer or poorer, better or worse, until death do them part. Yet as a couple recites their vows, they never honestly expect anything bad to happen. The couple is too caught up in the moment of a beautiful wedding ceremony to think of what can go wrong as they start a new life together. Rachelle and I were no different.

One afternoon when I was driving home from college, the Lord touched my heart that all of my wedding vows were going to be tested. When I arrived home, I hugged and kissed my new wife but never mentioned my thoughts to her. As I had lunch and prepared to leave for work that day, I knew without a doubt that the storm clouds were coming.

The winds and rain did come when two years later our son Paul was born. The adversities we faced shattered the dreams we had for him. One of the top five reasons why marriages end in divorce is due to children. Of those marriages that end in divorce due to children, a high percentage of them have a handicapped child. Yet Rachelle and I are still married after 30 years!

We certainly are not perfect people. Then how is it that we are still together even though we are still in this storm? My wife and I are very strong-willed people with strong opinions about everything. We are always honest, and neither one of us is afraid to speak our mind. Sometimes, that propensity leads to some very interesting discussions.

Life with a handicapped child is like a black hole that sucks up everything around it. It wasn't long after Paul was born that everything we did together was prefaced with the question, "What about Paul?"

Before he was born, we had plenty of time together for dates and romance. Now we both found ourselves trying to find the right balance between being good parents and good spouses. Paul's problems made it even more difficult to keep our marriage balanced. There were times when both of us felt neglected because Paul took up so much of our time.

The wedding vows that we exchanged have been the glue that keeps us together. There have been many times that I went alone with God and recited those vows while I lifted my left hand toward Heaven. I told the Lord that no matter how hard it became, I would one day stand before Him having kept my marriage pure. They were words that we obeyed—not just words that we said before we ate cake.

God's promises have been the guiding light and bedrock of our marriage during these years of constant trials. I am still amazed at how the Lord has never failed us in our times of need. Our trials and temptations are just as great now as they were then, but God is always good all the time.

Several years after my parents and siblings and I moved from Cypremort Point, my grandfather's house burned down. As we looked at the burned remains of his house, I noticed that the concrete pillars were still standing. I realize now that his house survived Hurricane Audrey because it was built on the right foundation. Our marriage still stands today because we purposed in our hearts that it was going to be built on the right foundation—our wedding vows and God's Word.

Still Sweethearts!

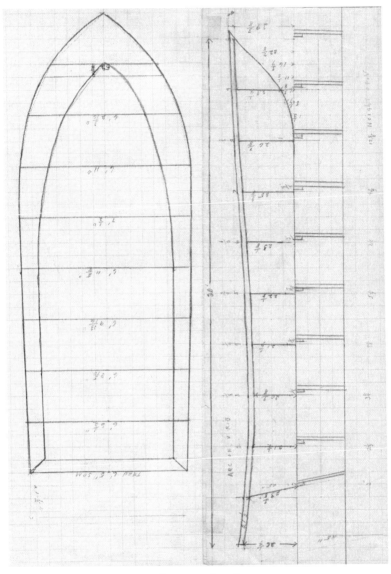

Above and right:
Drawings of Dad's boat project

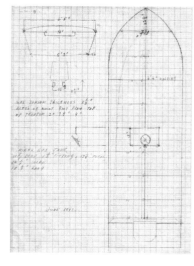

14

I Am Under Construction

"For we are his workmanship, created in Christ Jesus unto good works, which God hath before ordained that we should walk in them." (Ephesians 2:10)

SINCE THE SOUTH Louisiana economy was centered on the maritime industries, boat building played a major role in the livelihood of our people. My dad was not only a skilled tugboat captain, but also an excellent boat builder—a skill that he had learned from many of his relatives.

As a young boy, I watched in total amazement how Dad transformed a set of numbers that he had memorized into a beautiful boat. He always started with a small pencil drawing of the boat he had in mind to build. It was not uncommon for him to wear out a pencil eraser while he made constant modifications to the original sketches of the boat.

Once he was satisfied with the final drawings, he laid the keel for the boat in our back yard. After the keel was prop-

Above: Dad working on his boat

Below: The ribs of the boat

erly laid, he built the bow stem and transom. Then using the numbers he had memorized, he built a jig that formed the shape of the boat. Starting at the bow, Dad built each of the boat's individual ribs that fit precisely inside the jig.

After the ribs were completed, he boiled several long strips of wood in hot water inside a long pipe. The softened strips of wood were then bent and nailed to the ribs. The ribs were then covered with plywood. Slowly, after many months of work, the plans and raw lumber were transformed into a beautiful boat. The finished boat was my dad's workmanship.

The good works of the boat were fishing trips, catching shrimp, and providing boat rides with our family. When Dad looked at the drawings and numbers on the paper, he before ordained that we would go fishing in the boat. It was what he had in mind when he was looking at the plans for our boat.

We Are God's Workmanship.

Just as Dad had a purpose for the boat he built, God has a purpose for each one of us. In remembering all of the boats that Dad built, I realized I had learned several powerful lessons that I could apply to my life:

1. **Dad understood the plans.** Whenever Dad looked at his drawings, he understood what each of those numbers and lines meant. With that understanding of the drawings, he was able to execute the plans to build the boat. So it is with our lives. We do not always understand why God allows different circumstances into our lives, but we can trust Him to understand the plans that He will utilize to build our lives.

2. **Dad purchased the lumber.** Each piece of wood needed to build the boat was skillfully selected by my father. He did

not allow the workers in the lumberyard to pick the wood. The owner of the lumberyard had a large selection of wood available for my father, but Dad decided which pieces he wanted to purchase for the boat. I Corinthians 6:20, *"For ye are bought with a price: therefore glorify God in your body, and in your spirit, which are God's."*

3. Dad shaped the lumber according to his plans. Each piece of lumber was shaped and bent according to Dad's purpose for which it was selected. Some pieces of the lumber were used to build the ribs. Other pieces of wood were used for the transom and bow stem. No one piece of wood was always shaped like the other, but each one of them served a specific purpose in Dad's design.

We may not always like how God is shaping us, but we can be assured that He is shaping us according to His divine purpose. When the lumber yielded its properties to Dad, it was transformed into what he wanted it to be—a beautiful boat. Romans 12:1 and 2 says, *"I beseech you therefore, brethren, by the mercies of God, that ye present your bodies a living sacrifice, holy, acceptable unto God, which is your reasonable service. And be not conformed to this world: but be ye transformed by the renewing of your mind, that ye may prove what is that good, and acceptable, and perfect, will of God."*

4. The workmanship was necessary for the work. Dad's precise workmanship created a wonderful boat. The end result netted great fishing trips and boat rides with my family.

If Dad had used poor quality materials and done shoddy work, the boat would never have functioned and served the purpose for which it was planned. God's workmanship is the same way in our lives. Every trial we face is used by Him to execute His divine purpose for our lives. That is why the workmanship of God in our lives is needed for the good works He ordained for us to do.

Above inset: The finished boat!
Below: Mom and me sitting in Dad's boat

15

THE GROUP HOME

BECAUSE PAUL'S STAY at Silvercrest was temporary, we needed to find a permanent place for him. It was during the summer of 1989 when Rachelle met a friend from her college days after church. As they talked about Paul, Genevieve Atchison mentioned that her husband, Tom, worked with a local agency that managed group homes for autistic children and adults. The next week we scheduled an appointment with the agency.

We took copies of Paul's entire medical history with us for our first interview. Our first interview with the agency was very positive. We left copies of Paul's records with them for their review. After the agency examined his records, several workers from the agency went to Silvercrest to determine if Paul met the criteria for admission to one of the group homes.

It was during this time that Rachelle began having the constant headaches that led the doctors to discover the tumor in her brain. Her brain tumor changed the entire dynamics of our situation. Not only were we faced with finding a place for Paul, but we also faced an uncertain future about Rachelle. These questions and others like them constantly whirled in our minds.

- "What if the tumor is malignant?"
- "What if she doesn't survive the surgery?"

- "If she does survive the surgery, what about her physical abilities?"

These kind of questions with unknown answers added to the urgency to make some decisions about Paul. Looking back, I believe God used Rachelle's brain tumor to put Paul on the fast track to getting into the group home.

I will always be thankful to Tom and his agency for helping us to stay one step ahead of all the paperwork required by the other agencies which determined Paul's eligibility for the group home. Each agency required a certain form to be filled out in order to qualify for their services. Whenever we walked into any particular agency's office, the paperwork was already filled out. We were also ahead of the curve when Paul was enrolled in the Indiana Medicaid program. These actions on our part helped reduce the amount of time it took to get Paul qualified for the services he needed. After several meetings and further discussions, Paul was accepted into the agency's group home program.

Meanwhile, the agency had purchased a house in Hammond, Indiana. While the house was being remodeled, some of the neighbors learned it was going to be a home for autistic children. This discovery turned into a real battle with the neighbors, the city council, and the mayor. All of them refused to allow the group home to open. Tom assured us that everything would turn out in our favor. This was not the first time he had had to deal with local officials.

The mayor and the city council continued to oppose the opening of the new group home and used all of their political and legal clout against the agency. However, they did not realize that the U.S. Supreme Court had already ruled that no city or town could prevent handicapped people from living in their neighborhoods. Congress put some "teeth" into this decision by allowing the federal government to freeze all of a city's assets if they refused to obey the court's ruling. When the mayor's office received a phone call from the federal government that the city's assets were about to be frozen, he called Tom's agency and said, "Welcome to the neighborhood." God had wrought yet another miracle on our behalf.

16

Living in the Group Home

Now that the mayor and the city council had dropped their opposition, it was time to admit Paul into the new group home. Paul had to have another physical and psychological exam. Then the paperwork started. We had to sign permission and disclosure forms for everything. One form was for the medicines Paul was taking, and another form allowed the staff to take Paul to the doctors. Some of the forms gave Paul permission to participate in school activities and social events. Rachelle and I sat at the table as the forms kept being passed around. I don't believe there was any thought about saving the trees at this meeting.

Once the paperwork was finished, the time came to read all of Paul's evaluations and medical summaries. One by one each of the staff workers read their reports about Paul.

> "Today, we are here to admit Paul to the Forest Avenue group home. He is the son of Jad and Rachelle Terrebonne. He has one sister named Amy. He is a six-year-old Caucasian male with a diagnosis of autism and mental retardation."

Then it was time for the dietician to give her report. She went on and on about his height and weight and whether or not it was normal for his age. She then mentioned that Paul did not like milk but loved cheese and tolerated ice cream. He also liked pizza and hamburgers. Paul needed to be encouraged to eat his vegetables. When the meeting was over, I needed to be encouraged to eat my vegetables.

The quarterly and annual meetings that followed were vital in helping shape Paul's future. Rachelle and I participated in every one of them. We stayed on top of everything that happened and spoke up immediately when anything went wrong. The staff members were surprised at how involved we were with Paul. On one occasion the director told me that we were looked upon as "strange birds" because of our involvement with Paul's daily life. But none of them doubted how much we loved our son.

Rachelle was finishing the last couple of months of her physical therapy when the day came to move Paul into the group home. We had just celebrated Paul's seventh birthday. We were grateful that he was going to be closer to us. However, we were heartbroken that Paul would never again live in our home—apart from a miracle from God. When we arrived at the group home, Rachelle unpacked his clothes and placed them in the dresser drawers. She sat on the floor and wept uncontrollably.

We were concerned that the group home was not a Christian facility and that Paul would be attending a public school. From the outset, we had to take a stand on what he was allowed to see on television and what music was played. The staff at the group home were good people. We just did not share the same philosophy.

We also had to deal with people who did not understand why Paul was placed in a group home. From my experience, my

advice to families who are faced with this decision is threefold:
1. Do what is right for your marriage and your family.
2. Do not expect anyone to understand or agree with what you are doing.
3. Remember that you will always deal with people who think they have all the answers to your problems.

Whenever I think about the duct tape on the light switches and the refrigerator door, I know we made the right decision. Imagine what it would be like to live with a four-year-old boy who was strong enough to pull the handle off of the refrigerator door. When Paul was in his teenage years, he was strong enough to pull the fan from the ceiling in his bedroom.

Even though we wanted Paul to be in a Christian home, early intervention with his problems was vital to his development. We wanted Paul to reach his potential. I always felt like King Solomon holding a two-edged sword. It was a constant battle to balance the need to get help for Paul and to maintain our Christian convictions. My constant prayer was, "God, give me wisdom to bear the sword You placed in my hand!" These were some of the most heart-wrenching decisions we ever made.

After his admission to the Forest Avenue home, Paul made steady progress in his new environment. He and the other boys were trained to do a variety of chores around the house. Some of the boys had to take out the trash and learn to set the table for the daily meals. When the meal was finished, they had to clear off the table and load the dishwasher. Paul was taught how to wash and dry his own clothes. Each one of them had learn how to make his own bed.

The children were also taken out into the public and taught proper behavior. Trips to the grocery store were common. They learned how to select items from off of the shelf and place them in the grocery cart. When they arrived at the checkout counter, they had to take the groceries out of the cart and place them on the conveyor belts. The staff worked very hard in helping the boys learn to be self-sufficient.

Paul

The boys were also involved in many after-school activities. Paul joined a special ed baseball team. With proper coaching, he learned to hit the ball off of the tee and run the bases. At the end of the season, all of the participants were awarded trophies. He participated in the Special Olympics and enjoyed swimming and bowling. All the boys went on field trips to the museums and zoo. Paul was enjoying a well-rounded life.

One afternoon Tom called to tell us that the United Way was having their annual fund raiser and wanted to feature someone from the group home. Tom asked us if we wanted to participate in making the video. Rachelle and I agreed, and the next week someone from the local television station interviewed us about Paul.

After the interview, a camera crew came to the house and filmed us doing various activities around the house. We were then filmed taking a walk to the park behind our house with Paul pulling his red wagon. When we arrived at the park, we were filmed playing with the children on the swings.

Once the filming was finished, Rachelle and I went to the television studio to videotape our story. The director of the project had a script written based on the information we gave him during our first interview with him. We both sat in front of the camera as we read our script from the teleprompter. It took several takes to get it done because we were constantly getting tongue-tied as we read our scripts. When the video was televised, it became an instant success. United Way had the highest fund raiser in its history.

Paul enjoyed coming to church with us on Sunday. The Sunbeam Department at the First Baptist Church of Hammond was such a blessing. Paul loved singing all of the new songs he learned in Sunday school. Christian music was a major part in his life and helped him to have a good spirit. Even though he did not speak, he did sing clearly enough to be under-

Paul with Dr. Jack Hyles and Tom Atchison

stood. His love of church and Christian music did not set well with the public school teachers. One of his teachers said she was never able to start her class on Monday until Paul "had church" with everyone. Every Monday morning Paul sang all of the songs he had learned in Sunday school. Another teacher complained that she was afraid of losing her job if Paul did not quit singing about God during class time. On a couple of occasions, we felt she sent him home on some flimsy excuse just to keep him from singing about the Lord. We were glad to hear the news that she had stopped teaching to have a baby.

One Saturday Rachelle and Amy, along with one of Amy's friends, decided to stop at Paul's group home after a wedding they had attended at our church. When they arrived, Rachelle went to Paul's room. Amy and her friend stayed in the family room where the rest of the boys were being allowed to watch an inappropriate video. Amy told Rachelle what had happened. We called the parents of Amy's friend and apologized for the incident. On Monday we called the administration to report the incident. The worker who had rented the video was immediately dismissed from her job. Although this was a seemingly isolated incident, it was one of the many reasons we prayed that one day Paul could someday live in a Christian home.

During one of our annual meetings, we asked for Paul to be transferred to one of the Merrillville group homes. Our town was well-known for its special education department. Paul was ready to enter into junior high school, and we did not want him to attend an inner city school. After several meetings and discussions, Paul was transferred to a group home a few miles from our house.

17

TO MY BROTHER PAUL

Growing up, I often felt as if I were an only child. How could someone who could not talk, play, or do anything with me be my brother? Where were you when I wanted someone to play with? Where were you when I wanted to look cool and have you drive me to school like all the other kids? Where were you when I just wanted someone my age to talk to? Why couldn't you be normal? The attention was always on you, and I was jealous.

Amy's first Christmas

I remember going into your room and making you angry just so you would throw a fit, and I could "fight" with my big brother. I would sit on your bed and try to think of ways to play with you so I wouldn't be lonely. You would just look at me for a minute and go back to listening to your music. Every Christmas I would sneak into your room around 4:00 a.m. and wake you so we could pretend we were excited to open presents. Some years, after I would wake you up, I would make you

Amy and big brother Paul

go wake up Mom and Dad so we could open presents early, and I'd always blame it on you.

I can remember making you wash dishes with me because I didn't think it was fair you didn't have to; you would just stand there, and I would pretend to get angry at you because you wouldn't help.

When I started playing piano, I would make you come sit and listen to me play and pretend to enjoy it.

I would turn up the thermostat and tell Mom and Dad you did it so you could get in trouble. I just wasn't old enough to understand why you wouldn't

Piano awards

play with me. I knew you were handicapped, but why couldn't you just play with me?

I wanted so badly to be a part of your world. I wanted you to come to my room and ask me how your little sister was doing. I wanted to talk to you about dating and what we would do when we grew up. I was envious of all my friends who had siblings and would talk about their getting their driver's license, graduating, or dating. I would come home from school and walk by your room, wishing you were there to be my brother. I hated having to sit in the handicapped section at church. Why couldn't we sit where everyone else did?

Why didn't you come to any of my recitals, games, or graduation? Why is all I could ever ask and could never figure out?

I look back on my childhood now and realize how blessed I have been. Although I may not have a "normal" brother and someone to keep me company, I realize how privileged I really was. I was able to do everything growing up that you were never able to. You were never able to attend Hammond Baptist Schools. I wish you could know what an amazing school system I had the privilege of attending. You never got to be in our awesome youth group. You never got to play sports, date, or even drive.

I want you to realize how amazing Mom and Dad are. I know you see and hear them, but I do not think you can comprehend how they are. I have never met any two people so dedicated, hard-working, and loving as our parents. I wish you were able to see this side of them that I have been able to see all these years.

Our dad has worked at Community Hospital for almost 30 years and has gone through some incredible health issues, but he has always been there and provided for us. He has had carpal tunnel syndrome, meningitis, and so many health issues while we grew up. He has been a deacon at our church for 13 years. When times got tough, Dad was always there. I wish you could have gotten close to him. There were times growing up I had no idea what to do, and Dad would give me wisdom and help me through each situation. Dad is hilarious too; he has the corniest jokes and loves to poke fun, and he always makes you laugh. We are so blessed to call him Dad.

Above left: Paul and Amy
Above right: Amy's kindergarten graduation
Below left: My Uncle Charlie on the left with me, my dad and
Amy after a fishing trip
Below right: Amy and her graduate dad

Above left: Mrs. Hyles poses with Amy at the Science Fair
Above right: Dr. Hyles poses with Amy at a Blue Denim and
Lace event
Below left: Amy and Paul • Below right: Amy and her mom

Left: Amy, the cheerleader
Right: Amy at Hyles-Anderson College graduation

Then there is our amazing Mom. I hope someday you can understand how much she loves you. When you were five, she had a brain tumor and almost didn't live, but Mom is a fighter. She never gave up on you when everyone else did. She has fought for you to have a good home and to protect you all these years. When you were placed in home after home, every weekend she was there making sure you were taken care of. The second anything would come up, Mom was on the phone taking care of it and making sure you were treated right. When you were in the hospital, she was by your side every step of the way. I will never forget when you had a really bad seizure. Mom was on the phone in seconds getting an ambulance to the house. She held you through the whole seizure and continued to hold you as you rode in the back of the ambulance.

Mom is such a hard worker. She has really bad knees because of the surgery she had years ago, but that never stopped her from taking care of us all those years. She had a rough childhood, but you would never know that by the joy and happiness she portrays.

She is such a giver. All these years I teased her about loving you more because she was always there for you whenever you were in need. You see her laugh and may not understand, but she is hilarious. We'll be sitting at a casual dinner, and Dad will say something to her, and she has these laughing spells where she can't stop. Her laughter will continue for several minutes; it's so funny! Oh, and don't listen to her when she tries to make you say you like the Detroit Tigers! We Cub fans must stick together.

I love seeing you and spending time with you. Sometimes I get to stop by Mom and Dad's house on Monday nights, and I get a big hug from you. I wish you could know how much that hug means to me. I love when you come over on Saturday afternoons and eat lunch with Daniel and me. Thank you so much for being a groomsman in my wedding; you did such a good job of escorting Mom down the aisle!

Thank you for being such a wonderful brother and for being so patient with me. I am so proud of you, and I know God is too. You have overcome so much, and God knew how strong you would be to put you through this trial. Someday when we are both in Heaven, I want to catch up with you, my big brother. I want to talk to you about things you like, what your thoughts are, and how you feel.

I want you to know I will always be here for you and will never let you go to a home where they don't care or you are not

properly cared for. I will
always take care of you when
Mom and Dad are gone. I will
sacrifice what I need to make
sure you are happy.

I love you, Paul, and I am
so glad you are my brother.

Love, Amy

Paul and Amy ride the Sunday school bus
with Dr. Pete Cowling

18

WHAT ABOUT OUR FAMILY?

DURING THIS TIME, I was in and out of college. Managing our finances with the medical bills from Rachelle's surgery and trying to keep Amy in Hammond Baptist School was difficult, to say the least. In the end, we filed for bankruptcy.

We faced a lot of challenges during the years I was a student at Hyles-Anderson College. However, I knew that someday I was going to graduate. One Sunday night Pastor Hyles announced a meeting for anyone who might be interested in attending evening classes. Enough people attended the meeting that Hyles-Anderson Evening College was started.

Shortly after that, Dr. Darrell Moore made an appointment with me to discuss how many hours of classes I wanted to take. Just before he arrived, I made a pot of Louisiana French Roast coffee while Rachelle straightened the house.

When Dr. Moore arrived, we sat in the dining room. As we talked about the plans for evening college, Rachelle poured us a cup of coffee. I told him that I was going to take seven hours of classes because of my financial situation. We talked for a few minutes, and Dr. Moore agreed that I should go back to college part-time. Just as we finished talking, he took a drink of his coffee. He took one look at me and another look inside the cup. Without any further word, he finished his cup of coffee. I still laugh whenever I remember the look on his face when he tasted our strong Cajun coffee. After our meeting, I walked outside with Dr. Moore and watched him drive away. As he was leaving, I said to myself, "I'm going back to college full-time, and I am going to graduate."

Two years later I was sitting in the church auditorium wearing my cap and gown as Dr. Wendell Evans, now the president emeritus of Hyles-Anderson College, read the names of the 1993 Hyles-Anderson College graduates. Rachelle was sitting next to me wearing a white gown. I was thrilled to death when my name was called, and I walked to the platform of First Baptist Church where Dr. Hyles handed me my green diploma cover. When I walked to the other side of the platform to return to my seat, I held up the diploma with both hands and yelled, "Yeah!!" After I returned to my seat, I opened the diploma cover, and imagine my consternation when I saw the "sorry" sheet that read, "You have not received your diploma because you still have one remaining class to complete." I enrolled in summer school and completed the class. On August 13, 1993, I received my bachelor of science degree.

Shortly before I graduated, I scheduled an appointment with Pastor Hyles to discuss my future. He and I discussed various possibilities, and we agreed to have another appointment. On our second appointment, Rachelle accompanied me. All three of us talked some more, and Pastor decided to schedule one more appointment with me.

As I prayed about our future, I kept seeing the faces of my two children. Amy was already taking piano lessons and enrolled in "Blue Denim and Lace," a service club for third through sixth grade girls. I can still see her dressed in her blue uniform with the different pins she earned. She was also a cheerleader for one of the grade school basketball teams. Paul was firmly established at the group home and was doing well. I didn't want either of them to start over if I decided to move. Then I thought of Rachelle. If we moved, the burden of taking care of Paul and Amy would be placed directly on her—especially if I decided to pastor a church.

On my third appointment with Pastor Hyles, I told him that I realized my life was quite complicated and that he had veto power over any decision I wanted to make. He took one look at me and said, "Jad, I want you to stay and rear your family here at First Baptist Church." This last meeting with my pastor was the best 15 minutes I have ever spent in my life. I have no regrets about following his wisdom.

This decision allowed my family sink their roots deeply and also gave them the security they needed to prosper in God's will. It was my goal for Amy and Paul to reach their potential and to have their own identity. I did not want Amy to be hindered from succeeding in life because she had a handicapped brother. For this reason, I allowed her to participate in practically everything the school and church had to offer.

Whenever she would come home from school and ask, "Dad, can I go on this activity or can I join this?" I always gave her the same answer.

"Go for it!"

I strongly believe that God used these opportunities to help Amy gain the confidence she needed in her early years of school. I will always be grateful to the teachers at our school for the Godly influence they had on her. While we were driving home from school one day, Amy looked at me and said, "Dad, I want to be a school teacher when I grow up."

The annual candy sales at the grade school were a major event in our life. The children were very competitive when it came to prizes that were available. One year Rachelle and I teamed up with Amy to help her win a trip to Washington, D.C.

The Blue Denim and Lace club provided Amy with the opportunity to learn a lot of practical skills. One by one she earned each of the 44 pins that Blue Denim and Lace had to offer. With that, she won all of the awards that came with earning the pins, including the pastor's study award, the pastor's home tour award, and the pastor's banquet award. The girls had the opportunity to earn the pastor's home tour and pastor's study award each year they were in the club. Amy enjoyed many visits with Brother Hyles. The pastor's banquet award was given only to the girls who completed all the work required for the 44 pins. On some of these visits, he hosted all of the girls at the college Hylander Lanes and bowled with them. He personally hosted the pastor's banquet award winners on the *S.S. Beverly*, on the lake at Hyles-Anderson College.

Piano lessons allowed music to shape Amy's life. She joined the children's choir, and when she entered junior high was chosen to be in the girl's ensemble. Her singing and piano playing gave her the emotional outlet she needed in dealing with Paul. Amy started taking lessons when she was in fifth grade until she was in her second year of college. Today she is an accomplished pianist.

While she was still in grade school, Amy started riding the bus to church. The bus ministry became a big part of her life. God used this as a tool to help her reach out to other people who were going through tough times.

As the school years went by, Amy made a lot of wonderful friends. It is interesting to note that two of her closest friends did not have sisters. Throughout their school years, they were considered the three amigos.

She saw the challenges of the science and history fairs in junior high school. Her first science fair project was on the subject of blood. Since I was working in the laboratory at the hospital, she received a lot of help from dear old Dad. I took her on a tour of our lab while we took a lot pictures. That year she won first place on her project.

Teenage soul winning was part of her Saturday routine. It may sound strange, but all of the candy sales she participated in gave her confidence to become a good soul winner. By the time she graduated from Hammond Baptist High School, she had led over 1,000 people to Christ.

I watched Amy mature during her high school years. I was continually impressed as she surrounded herself with the right kind of friends. They were always pulling for each other during difficult times. She was also in musical ensembles throughout her four years in high school. The highlight of her senior year was being chosen as a cheerleader.

During her senior year of high school, I had a father-daughter talk with Amy. I reminded her not to let unforeseen events becoming a stumbling block in her last year of school. I went on to explain that the anticipation of her graduation could be overshadowed by an unexpected event.

When Amy was in the fourth grade, my father was in a severe boating accident. He survived the accident, but his health was rapidly deteriorating. Just two weeks before Amy graduated from high school, Dad went to Heaven.

Upon graduation from high school, she enrolled in Hyles-Anderson College and majored in elementary education. She spent four years taking a full load of classes while holding down a full-time job. On top of her classes and job, she spent her weekends working in the bus ministry.

During her sophomore year, she started dating a young man from South Carolina. I was impressed that Amy learned Southern-style cooking. They continued dating through her remaining years in college.

In May of 2007, Amy graduated from Hyles-Anderson College. As I watched her walk across the platform to receive her degree, I remembered all of the years watching her grow up, and I thanked God I had followed my preacher's advice and had stayed here at First Baptist Church. Soon after she graduated, Rachelle and I were surprised to hear that Amy was hired to teach at City Baptist Grade School. It was one of the proudest moments of our lives.

Then on November 1, 2008, at 2:00 in the afternoon, Amy Rachelle Terrebonne became Mrs. Daniel Beck Luarca. Her wedding was a wonderful day for Rachelle and me. When I placed her hand in Daniel's arm, I knew Rachelle and I were giving her to God's will for her life. Daddy's little girl had grown up.

Above left: Paul and Amy; Halloween time
Above right: Paul and Amy; Christmas
Below left: Amy and Dad with Muffin
Below right: the "three amigos"—Amy with her friends,
Amy Ossewaarde and Janel Flesher

Above: Amy with Aunt Starr, Uncle Maynard, Aunt Sherry
Below: Amy and Daniel

Above: Amy and Daniel; just married!
Below: Amy and Rachelle

Above:
Family Photo: Dad,
Daniel, Amy, Paul,
and Rachelle

Below:
Amy and Dad

19

MOVING TO MERRILLVILLE

THE YEARS THAT Paul spent at the Forest Avenue Group Home laid a good foundation for him at the Seventy-Eighth Avenue Group Home in Merrillville. The administrator of the group home, Dorothy, was known for running a tight ship at the Merrillville home, and Paul was not going to be an exception to her rules. Once he had adjusted to his new surroundings, Paul was given his list of duties and expected to tow the line like everyone else. Dorothy had a real heart for these boys and treated them as if they were her very own. Within a few weeks, Paul had adjusted to his new environment.

After a year at the junior high school, Paul was transferred to Merrillville High School. We met annually to review his educational goals and planned for the upcoming year. His teacher learned that Paul enjoyed activities that required a lot of walking around. She decided to have him take the daily attendance sheet to the principal's office. Each of the forms was a different color. His teacher then mixed up the forms, and Paul had to correctly identify the attendance sheet before he took it to the principal's office. To his credit, Paul needed directions only one time before he was able to go to the office by himself.

Now that Paul was getting older, his behavior in public was crucial. He was not allowed to touch himself inappropriately.

He was also taught how to greet people by shaking hands instead of grabbing them with a bear hug. This training was vital at this stage of his life. He was expected to behave like a young adult.

He was issued an official state identification card to carry in his wallet. He had to show it to various people when they asked for it. His name, address, and photograph were given to the local police in case of an emergency.

Paul had a hearty appetite; however, he constantly gobbled down his food. This is because autistic people do not like to touch their lips. Specialists believe that the sensation of food on the lips helps control the volume or amount that is placed in the mouth. On one of our trips to McDonalds, I had to return to the counter to get some condiments. By the time I returned, Paul had already eaten his entire hamburger in two bites.

His teacher shared various methods of helping Paul slow down while he ate. He had to put down his fork after each bite of food and wipe his lips. He also had to take a drink of water before his next bite of food. Imagine our conversation around the dinner table: "Small bite, Paul."

"Honey, how was your day? Wipe your lips, Paul."

"Busy day at work? Take a drink, Paul."

"Amy did you have a good week at school? Small bite, Paul. Now take a drink."

One day during lunch, Paul's teacher held up one finger and said, "Paul, one French fry." Paul proceeded to stuff several of them into his mouth. His teacher immediately threw the rest of the fries in the trash can. She had Paul's full attention. The next day during lunch, Paul looked at his teacher as he held up one finger and said, "One fry."

We pushed for Paul to have speech therapy as much as possible. Paul's rapid method of speaking sounds like high-speed mumbling. When I picked him up for his weekend visits, he said, "Took out the garbage! Took out the garbage, yeah!" Paul was given a dynavox voice box with a lot of pictures on it. Whenever he touched a picture, the voice box stated the word he wanted to express. However, we had very little success with this device.

Music remained a large part of his life. When he wasn't listening to Patch the Pirate, he loved to listen to Walt Disney sing-along videos. One afternoon, Paul was listening to the song Zip-a-Dee-Doo-Dah.

"Zip-a-dee-doo-dah, zip-a-dee-day,
My, oh my, what a wonderful day
Plenty of sunshine headin' my way
Zip-a-dee-doo-dah, zip-a-dee-ay."

Somehow this song managed to become drilled into my memory, and on more than one occasion, I found myself singing, "Zip-a-dee-doo-dah, zip-a-dee-day," while I was walking down the hallway at work.

20

GRADUATION DAY

P AUL GRADUATED FROM Merrillville High School on June 9, 2005. This achievement was another step forward for him. Paul was now ready to step into an adult world. The following Saturday we went to a graduation party for him as well as for the other boys who had graduated with him. We enjoyed meeting some of the other parents while we enjoyed the great barbeque feast that was provided by the staff.

The graduate and his sister

Now that he was finished with high school, it was time to be transferred to another group home. We were told that this would be the last time he would to be transferred. Rachelle and I both knew that we would be faced with the same conflicts between our Christian beliefs and the agency's outlook. This time our differences of opinion would create a greater conflict now that Paul was an emancipated adult. Some of the staff at the group home were

constantly pushing Paul to make his own choices without any intervention on our part.

We did not realize that God was preparing the answer for us when John Wilson and his wife Diane knocked on our door one rainy night. While we sat at the dining room table, John outlined his ideas for helping us with Paul. The state of Indiana had an adult foster care program that would pay John to care for Paul. Since the program had few regulations, we had more discretion in how we wanted to care for our son. John had over 30 years of experience working with handicapped people. He had also worked in the Pathfinder Department of our church for over 18 years. We were amazed that God might be answering our prayers.

After our meeting with John, we scheduled an appointment with Pastor Schaap. Even though we liked the idea of John's caring for Paul, we wanted to make sure that this was going to benefit everyone involved. During the course of our discussion, Pastor Schaap said, "I would rather work with the devil I know than with the devil I don't know." With his wisdom and advice, we decided to go forward with the idea.

Our biggest roadblock was getting Paul a Medicaid waiver slot. Paul was already on the waiting list. The state opened a few slots every year, and hundreds of people were on the list. To make matters worse, the state of Indiana was in a budget crisis. In order to get Paul into the foster care program, we needed to find funding outside the Medicaid waiver program.

The idea of placing Paul into the adult foster care program created a firestorm within the agency. Some of the managers were opposed to the idea while others voiced their support on our behalf. However, we did work hard at being diplomatic with everyone, including the key players who were against us. When diplomacy failed, we stood firm and made our case for Paul.

Knowing that the odds were against us, we applied to the state for the funding we needed to place Paul in the foster care program. Several weeks later we were turned down. We applied for funding under another program and were turned down again.

Rachelle started calling various agencies in Indianapolis. She pleaded our case to as many people as were willing to listen. She contacted the Family and Social Services Agency and spoke to the assistant director of that agency. She called the governor's office and spoke with his secretary.

We wrote a letter to the governor's office and outlined the cost effectiveness of the program. We discovered that it cost the state of Indiana almost $100,000 a year to care for Paul in the group home. The adult foster care cost approximately $35,000 a year. We also wrote to our state senator. We worked for a whole year to get Paul approved for the program. Throughout this time, we enlisted people from our church to pray. We contacted Dr. Tom Williams and asked him to pray. Pastor Schaap also prayed with us. The throne of Heaven was bathed in prayer.

The day came for our final meeting at the agency. The answer from Indianapolis was a resounding No. We were told to try again in five to ten years. However, Rachelle and I both knew that it was now or never with Paul. We were determined not to give up, and we kept on pushing forward.

Once again our hearts were lifted up to God in prayer. I told Rachelle that we needed a special promise from the Bible that God would give us the answer we needed. I opened my Bible to Luke 1:37, *"For with God nothing shall be impossible,"* and claimed the verse for Paul. Two weeks later we received a letter in the mail from the state of Indiana. The letter stated that Paul was approved for an autism Medicaid waiver. God had miraculously answered our prayers!

Through the years, our faith has been constantly tested. Many times our faith has failed or even languished. Yet through the entire time the Lord has always been faithful. *"Now unto him that is able to do exceeding abundantly above all that we ask or think, according to the power that worketh in us, Unto him be glory in the church by Christ Jesus throughout all ages, world without end. Amen."* (Ephesians 3:20, 21) God answered our prayers for Paul after 20 years of praying, yet we realize that the journey is not over.

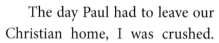

21

A Mother's Point of View

I TOO WANTED A normal son. Like any other mother, I wanted Paul to grow and prosper like other children. But God had other plans. Twenty-six years later I still do not understand all of the reasons why Paul is handicapped, but I do know that God is always good. I look forward to the day when Paul has a glorified body and can tell me all that is in his heart.

Mom and Son

The day Paul had to leave our Christian home, I was crushed. "What am I to do?" I agonized. I was facing brain surgery and an uncertain future. Paul needed more help than we were able to give him. Yet God was faithful in providing the experts we needed to help Paul reach his potential.

Because he had lived in a Christian home and attended church with us, Paul loved the songs of our faith. However, due to the philosophies of the public schools and other world-ly influences, he stopped singing these songs. It became very obvious that Paul was not able to enjoy his Christianity at the group home. It was important to my husband and me that

Paul would grow spiritually. From the first day Paul moved into the group home, we prayed that one day he would live in a Christian home.

The night that John and Diane came to our house and shared their burden with us about Paul, my heart was filled with joy. God was answering our prayers. Paul has been with them almost four years. He is now singing the songs he learned as a boy. John found a hat for him that says, "God is good all the time." It is a blessing to see Paul express his faith again. Now Paul tells everyone he sees, "God is good to me all the time, and Jesus loves you too."

I also want to share some of the many verses that the Lord has used to give me hope and strength.

- *"But he knoweth the way that I take: when he hath tried me, I shall come forth as gold."* (Job 23:10)

- *"And he said unto me, My grace is sufficient for thee: for my strength is made perfect in weakness. Most gladly therefore will I rather glory in my infirmities, that the power of Christ may rest upon me. Therefore I take pleasure in infirmities, in reproaches, in necessities, in persecutions, in distresses for Christ's sake: for when I am weak, then am I strong."* (II Corinthians 12:9, 10)

- *"Now unto him that is able to do exceeding abundantly above all that we ask or think, according to the power that worketh in us."* (Ephesians 3:20)
- *"Behold, I will do a new thing; now it shall spring forth; shall ye not know it? I will even make a way in the wilderness, and rivers in the desert."* (Isaiah 43:19)

I am also compiling a book of poems and prose about handicapped children. The following three are very meaningful to me:

Welcome to Holland

by Emily Perl Kingsley

I am often asked to describe the experience of raising a child with a disability to try to help people who have not shared that unique experience to understand it, to imagine how it would feel.

It's like this…
When you're going to have a baby,
It's like planning a fabulous vacation trip—to Italy.
You buy a bunch of guide books and make your wonderful plans.
The Coliseum. The Michelangelo David. The gondolas in Venice.
You may learn some handy phrases in Italian. It's all very exciting.

After months of eager anticipation, the day finally arrives.
You pack your bags and off you go.
Several hours later, the plane lands.
The stewardess comes in and says,
"Welcome to Holland."

"Holland?!?" you say. "What do you mean Holland??
I signed up for Italy! I'm supposed to be in Italy.
All my life I've dreamed of going to Italy."
But there's been a change in the flight plan.
They've landed in Holland, and there you must stay.

The important thing is that they haven't taken you to a horrible, disgusting, filthy place, full of pestilence, famine and disease.

It's just a different place.

So you must go out and buy new guide books.

And you must learn a whole new language.

And you will meet a whole new group of people you would never have met.

It's just a different place.

It's slower-paced than Italy, less flashy than Italy.

But after you've been there for a while and you catch your breath, you look around...and you begin to notice that Holland has windmills...and Holland has tulips.

Holland even has Rembrandts.

But everyone you know is busy coming and going from Italy...and they're all bragging about what a wonderful time they had there.

And for the rest of your life, you will say

"Yes, that's where I was supposed to go.

That's what I had planned."

And the pain of that will never, ever, ever, ever go away... because the loss of that dream is a very, very significant loss.

But...if you spend your life mourning the fact that you didn't get to Italy, you may never be free to enjoy the very special, the very lovely things...about Holland.

What You Should Know About My Child
– Author Unknown

Remember that he is, first of all, my child.

Let me see him smiling in his sleep and let me think about how handsome he is and not about how delayed that smile was in coming.

Help me not lose sight of my son in the shadow of his limitations.

I know that you care for my child and that you work hard with him.

I need your expertise to help him become all that he is capable of being.

You need my help in understanding who he really is and in following through at home with things that are important.

Remember, though, that you send him home at night and have weekends off and paid vacations.

Let me have the luxury of having a vacation, sometimes physically, sometimes just emotionally, for a day, a week, a month, without your judging me.

I will be there for him when you are long gone.

I love my child with an intensity that you can only imagine.

If on a given day I am tired or cross with him, listen to me, lighten my burden, but do not judge me.

Celebrate with me, rejoice in who he is and who he will become but forgive me if from time to time I shed a tear for who he might have been.

I Am the Child

I am the child who cannot talk.

You often pity me, I see it in your eyes.

You wonder how much I am aware of—I see that as well.

I am aware of much, whether you are happy or sad or fearful, patient or impatient, full of love and desire, or if you are just doing your duty by me.

I marvel at your frustration, knowing mine to be far greater, for I cannot express myself or my needs as you do.

You cannot conceive my isolation, so complete it is at times.

I do not gift you with clever conversation, cute remarks to be laughed over and repeated.

I do not give you answers to your everyday questions, responses over my well-being, sharing my needs, or comments about the world about me.

I do not give you rewards as defined by the world's standards—great strides in development that you can credit yourself;

I do not give you understanding as you know it.

What I give you is so much more valuable—I give you instead opportunities.

Opportunities to discover the depth of your character, not mine;

The depth of your love, your commitment, your patience, your abilities; the opportunity to explore your spirit more deeply than you imagined possible.

I drive you further than you would ever go on your own, working harder, seeking answers to your many questions with no answers.

I am the child who cannot talk.

I am the child who cannot walk.

The world seems to pass me by.

You see the longing in my eyes to get out of this chair, to run and play like other children.

There is much you take for granted.

I want the toys on the shelf; I need to go to the bathroom; oh, I've dropped my fork again.

I am dependent on you in these ways.

My gift to you is to make you more aware of your great fortune, your healthy back and legs, your ability to do for yourself.

Sometimes people appear not to notice me; I always notice them.

I feel not so much envy as desire, desire to stand upright, to put one foot in front of the other, to be independent.

I give you awareness.

I am the child who cannot walk.

I am the child who is mentally impaired.

I don't learn easily, if you judge me by the world's measuring stick; what I do know is infinite joy in simple things.

I am not burdened as you are with the strifes and conflicts of a more complicated life.

My gift to you is to grant you the freedom to enjoy things as a child, to teach you how much your arms around me mean, to give you love.

I give you the gift of simplicity.

I am the child who is mentally impaired.

I am the disabled child.

I am your teacher. If you allow me, I will teach you what is really important in life.

I will give you and teach you unconditional love.

I gift you with my innocent trust, my dependency upon you.

I teach you about how precious this life is and about not taking things for granted.

I teach you about forgetting your own needs and desires and dreams.

I teach you giving.

Most of all I teach you hope and faith.

I am the disabled child.

THANK YOU...

Jad, my husband, thank you for your love, patience, endurance, courage, grit, spunk, tolerance, understanding, and strength for me and our family. I couldn't have made it without you. Thank you for writing this book. And thank you for your wisdom about Paul. I LOVE YOU!!!

In closing, we hope you understand our hearts and motives while you read this book. May it be a blessing to you and a testimony to the goodness and greatness of our God.

22

PAUL MOVES TO A CHRISTIAN HOME

A FTER THE USUAL paperwork and meetings, Paul was able to move into the home of John and Diane Wilson. Again he had to adjust to his new environment. One day Paul decided to run away while he was dressed in his pajamas. Several minutes later he was found walking in the middle of Broadway Avenue. When the police arrived to help him, Paul started struggling with the officers and ended up in handcuffs. But as the weeks went by, he managed to settle down in his new home.

Now that Paul is living in a Christian home, his entire spirit is improving. He is also being challenged to be more self-reliant. He now attends church three times a week and sits with us in the main auditorium. Paul opens the song book at the right time and sings with us.

John is working with him about talking at the wrong times. He made a card with three pictures of French fries on it. Any time Paul misbehaves or speaks out of turn during the church service, an "X" is placed on the picture of the French fries. Once three X's are placed on the pictures, Paul will not get any fries after church.

In the morning before work, Paul has to shave himself and make his own bed before breakfast. One morning Paul was taking his time getting ready for breakfast. Diane had his plate ready as they sat and waited for Paul. Their dog sensed that Paul was taking his good old time, so he walked up to Paul's plate and ate his breakfast. Paul had to settle for a bowl of cold cereal and milk. The next morning Paul was up and ready for breakfast on time.

Paul is not allowed to just point at anything he wants. He has to verbally say what he wants before he gets it. During meal times, he has to finish his meal and ask for dessert in order to get it. John also found a way to slow Paul's eating by giving him a small salad fork to use during mealtime.

Paul is now learning to speak in complete sentences. One night he did not want to sit still while I brushed his teeth. After I scolded him and told him to sit still, he said, "Yeah, and Jesus loves you too." Rachelle and I took him out to eat one night. Paul walked up to a lady at the salad bar and said, "God is good to me all the time."

Paul is also a Chicago Cubs fan—much to my wife's disappointment! Recently he was able to tell us that the Cubs defeated the Chicago White Sox five to four.

A few weeks ago while I was getting Paul ready for work, I told him, "We are going to make you look nice for the girls."

Paul replied, "Girls, yeah!"

It is a joy and an honor to work with a Christian family who shares our values. There is no longer a conflict over what we want for Paul and what his caretakers want for him. We are all on the same page. Paul is allowed to express his faith in God. When Paul was living in the group home, he was allowed to attend church with us, but he was never encouraged to talk about God at the home.

A year later our church opened a thrift store. Through a

series of events, the agency that cared for Paul negotiated an agreement with our church to let some of the handicapped adults work there. Paul was already in another workshop that we felt was not giving him what he needed. We made a few phone calls, and Paul was transferred to our thrift store. Paul is now living and working entirely in a Christian environment.

Our journey with Paul is not over. We believe that God has big plans for his future. It is our hope and prayer that one day God will provide a permanent place for Paul and others like him. Please pray with us as the Lord takes us to the next level.

As I look back over the last 27 years of our life with Paul, it has been an incredible journey of faith, love, and perseverance. It would take another book to testify of every little thing that God has done for our son. To date, the Lord has provided nearly $2 million for the care of Paul. Revelation 4:11 says, *"Thou art worthy, O Lord, to receive glory and honour and power: for thou hast created all things, and for thy pleasure they are and were created."*

All I can say is, "To God be the glory, great things He hath done."

Above left: Paul enjoys his lunch.
Above right: Paul decorates a tree.
Below left: Paul at his job
Below right: John and Diane Wilson with Paul

*Above left: Cindy Mercer, the pianist in the Pathfinder
Department
Above right: Tom and Genevieve Atchison
Below: Ben Walkup, Paul's Sunday School teacher*

Above: Paul with Tina Webb and Leslie Giesler

How to Know for Sure You Are Going to Heaven

GOD HAS BEEN good to my family through the years. The main source of our strength and faith is that we trusted Jesus Christ as our personal Saviour. Trusting Christ is the one and only way to get to Heaven when we die. Jesus said in John 14:6, *"...I am the way, the truth, and the life: no man cometh to the Father, but by me."*

Let me share my own testimony of my salvation. One Sunday I attended the chapel services at the Naval hospital where I was stationed in Beaufort, South Carolina. The chaplain preached from the verse in John 8:32, *"And ye shall know the truth, and the truth shall make you free."* He went on to say that the truth will not always make your life easier or happier, but it will make you free. I left the service that day and said to myself, "I am going to find that truth he is talking about."

After several weeks, I discovered a Gideons' Bible in one of the filing cabinets while I was on duty at the dispensary one night. I took it to the pharmacy and closed the door behind me. I opened the Bible and found Deuteronomy 4:29 underlined by someone who had read it before me. *"But if from thence thou shalt seek the LORD thy God, thou shalt find him, if thou seek him with all thy heart and with all thy soul."* I closed the Bible and prayed, "Dear God, please show me the meaning of this verse." God was teaching me that my faith in Him had to come from my heart.

Not long after that prayer, I read a book about the second coming of Jesus Christ. At the end of the book, the author explained that Jesus Christ died on the Cross to pay for my sins. He cited Revelation 3:20, *"Behold, I stand at the door and knock: if any man hear my voice, and open the door, I will come in to him, and will sup with him, and he with me."* After I finished reading that chapter, I finally understood what the chaplain was saying about the truth and the meaning of Deuteronomy 4:29. Then I realized that in order to go to Heaven when I die, I had to believe with my heart that Jesus Christ was the only way to get to Heaven. The following Sunday I attended a church outside the gate of the Naval hospital. At the end of the service, I trusted Christ as my Saviour.

God loves you and wants you to know for sure that one day you will go to Heaven when you die. I John 5:13 says, *"These things have I written unto you that believe on the name of the Son of God; that ye may know that ye have eternal life, and that ye may believe on the name of the Son of God."*

God want us to understand several facts about our time on earth and our eternity after we die:

THE BIBLE SAYS WE ARE ALL SINNERS.

Romans 3:23 says, *"For all have sinned, and come short of the glory of God."* That verse means that no matter how good we may be, we are all sinners before God. Every one of us is guilty of having sinned against God. Romans 3:10 states, *"As it is written, There is none righteous, no, not one."* Again, not one individual is righteous enough to stand before God.

The penalty for sin is death.

"For the wages of sin is death; but the gift of God is eternal life through Jesus Christ our Lord." (Romans 6:23)

"Wherefore, as by one man sin entered into the world, and death by sin; and so death passed upon all men, for that all have sinned." (Romans 5:12) When Adam and Eve sinned against God, the curse of sin and death passed upon all mankind. There are two kinds of death: the physical death of our bodies and the spiritual death of our souls.

Revelation 21:8 explains, *"But the fearful, and unbelieving, and the abominable, and murderers, and whoremongers, and sorcerers, and idolaters, and all liars, shall have their part in the lake which burneth with fire and brimstone: which is the second death."* The second death occurs in the Lake of Fire or Hell. Everyone on earth who has not trusted Christ as his Saviour is destined for this Lake of Fire.

Jesus paid the price for our sins when He died on the Cross.

Romans 5:6 says, *"For when we were yet without strength, in due time Christ died for the ungodly."* Notice how the verse says that Christ died for the ungodly. Simply stated, it means that we are all ungodly. Romans 5:8, *"But God commendeth his love toward us, in that, while we were yet sinners, Christ died for us."* This verse means that God demonstrated His love toward us by sending His only begotten Son, Jesus Christ, to pay the penalty for our sins when He died on the Cross.

WE HAVE TO TRUST JESUS CHRIST AS OUR SAVIOUR AS THE ONLY HOPE TO GET TO HEAVEN.

Romans 10:9 and 10 says, *"That if thou shalt confess with thy mouth the Lord Jesus, and shalt believe in thine heart that God hath raised him from the dead, thou shalt be saved. For with the heart man believeth unto righteousness; and with the mouth confession is made unto salvation."*

Romans 10:13 says, *"For whosoever shall call upon the name of the Lord shall be saved."* Notice how these verses keep saying that we have to believe in Christ with our hearts. What we believe in our hearts, God wants us to confess with our mouths—our faith in Jesus Christ.

If you are willing to receive Jesus Christ as your Saviour, all you have to do is believe in your heart this simple prayer:

> "Dear Jesus, I know that I am a sinner. I know I deserve to die for my sins. Please forgive my sins. Thank You for dying in my place on the Cross and for rising from the dead at the end of three days. I trust You, Lord Jesus, to be my Saviour and only hope to get to Heaven when I die."

If you believe in your heart this simple prayer, the Bible says that you are now saved and on your way to Heaven. You are no longer under the curse of death but rather have the gift of eternal life. Romans 6:23 says, *"For the wages of sin is death; but the gift of God is eternal life through Jesus Christ our Lord."* Notice that we all deserve death because of sin, but we now have that wonderful gift of eternal life through Jesus Christ.

Jesus said in John 5:24, *"...He that heareth my word, and believeth on him that sent me, hath everlasting life, and shall not come into condemnation; but is passed from death unto life."* It means that when we hear and believe the Word of God concerning salvation, our sentence of eternal death is changed to everlasting life in Heaven with God.

We are now called His children. I John 2:1 says, *"My little children, these things write I unto you, that ye sin not. And if any man sin, we have an advocate with the Father, Jesus Christ the righteous."* Romans 8:16 says, *"The Spirit itself beareth witness with our spirit, that we are the children of God."*

Now that we are His children, we are accepted into His family. Ephesians 1:5, 6, *"Having predestinated us unto the adoption of children by Jesus Christ to himself, according to the good pleasure of his will, To the praise of the glory of his grace, wherein he hath made us accepted in the beloved. In whom we have redemption through his blood, the forgiveness of sins, according to the riches of his grace."* Once we are saved, the Bible says that we are accepted into His beloved family through Jesus Christ, His Son.